Better Homes and Gardens

so good with FRUIT

MEREDITH PRESS

NEW YORK   DES MOINES

CONTENTS

Fruit Medley Elegante mingles peaches, pears, strawberries, and bananas and is spiked with a mixture of
ruby red wine and citrus juices. This dazzling fruit compote can either top off a meal or begin a noonday brunch.

BEVERAGES
AND
APPETIZERS

Fill scalloped ivy-twined
watermelon shell
with Tropical Punch or any
delicious chilly
fruit punch. Appetizers made
with fruit will also
star as dinner-beginners.

Refreshing fruit drinks

TROPICAL PUNCH

1 large watermelon
1 46-ounce can (about 6 cups) red Hawaiian fruit punch
1 6-ounce can frozen pink lemonade concentrate
1 6-ounce can frozen orange juice concentrate
1 6-ounce can frozen pineapple juice concentrate
6 cups cold water
1 1-pint 12-ounce bottle (3½ cups) ginger ale, chilled

Stand watermelon on end; cut thin slice off bottom to make it level. Cut top third off melon. Using cup as guide, trace scallops around top outside edge of melon. Carve scalloped edge, following pattern. Scoop out fruit; serve later. Chill melon shell.

Combine Hawaiian fruit punch, fruit juice concentrates, and water. Pour over ice in melon bowl. Resting bottle on rim of melon, carefully pour ginger ale down side; mix with up-and-down motion. Float orange and lime slices. Twine melon with ivy leaves, holding with toothpicks. Makes 30 to 35 servings.

PUNCH FOR THE CROWD

3 quarts unsweetened pineapple juice
1½ cups lemon juice
3 cups orange juice
⅓ cup lime juice
2½ cups sugar
1 cup mint leaves
4 1-pint 12-ounce bottles ginger ale, chilled
2 1-pint 12-ounce bottles carbonated water, chilled
1 pint fresh strawberries, sliced

Combine juices, sugar, and mint leaves; chill several hours. Strain. Pour over large cake of ice in punch bowl. Resting bottle on rim of bowl, carefully pour in ginger ale and carbonated water; add strawberries. Float thin slices of lemon and lime. Serves 75.

FROSTY GOLDEN PUNCH

Great timesaver—canned juices form make-ahead base; sherbet and ginger ale add finishing touch—

1 6-ounce can frozen lemonade concentrate
1 6-ounce can frozen orange juice concentrate
1 6-ounce can frozen pineapple juice concentrate
1 12-ounce can (1½ cups) apricot nectar, chilled
½ cup lemon juice
1 quart lemon sherbet
2 1-pint 12-ounce bottles (7 cups) ginger ale, chilled

Add water to frozen concentrates according to directions on cans. Add apricot nectar and lemon juice. Just before serving, spoon in sherbet; rest bottle on rim and carefully pour ginger ale down side of bowl. Mix with up-and-down motion. Makes 20 to 25 servings.

CRANBERRY-CHERRY PUNCH

Cherry-flavored gelatin gives a new twist!

1 3-ounce package cherry-flavored gelatin
1 cup boiling water

. . .

1 6-ounce can frozen lemonade concentrate
3 cups cold water
1 1-quart bottle cranberry-juice cocktail, chilled
1 1-pint 12-ounce bottle (3½ cups) ginger ale, chilled

Dissolve gelatin in boiling water. Stir in lemonade concentrate. Add cold water and cranberry-juice cocktail. Place two trays of ice cubes or molded ice ring in large punch bowl. Pour punch over ice.

Resting bottle on rim of bowl, slowly pour ginger ale down side; mix with up-and-down motion. If desired, add scoops of fruit-flavored sherbet. Makes about 25 servings.

ORANGE EGGNOG

1 pint vanilla ice cream
½ 6-ounce can (⅓ cup) frozen
orange juice concentrate
1 egg
2 cups milk
Ground nutmeg

Blend ice cream, orange juice concentrate, and egg with electric mixer or rotary beater. Gradually add milk, beating constantly. Serve in chilled mugs with a sprinkle of nutmeg on top. Makes about 4 cups of eggnog.

Fresh and cool as a sea breeze—Old-time Lemonade sports striped sippers and perky trim of mint sprigs, lemon slices.

RHUBARB-LEMONADE PUNCH

2 12-ounce packages frozen
rhubarb
¼ to ½ cup sugar
1 6-ounce can frozen lemonade
concentrate
3 cups water
2 7-ounce bottles lemon-lime
carbonated beverage, chilled

In saucepan, combine frozen rhubarb, sugar, frozen lemonade concentrate, and water; cover and cook about 20 minutes, or till rhubarb is very soft. Strain to remove pulp; chill the liquid. Just before serving, pour rhubarb mixture over ice cubes in punch bowl. Resting bottle on rim of bowl, carefully pour in carbonated beverage. Makes 12 servings.

LIME FROSTED PUNCH

3½ to 4 cups pineapple-
grapefruit drink, chilled
⅔ cup lemon juice
2 quarts cold water
3 ½-ounce envelopes unsweetened
lemon-lime soft drink powder
2 cups sugar

. . .

2 pints lime sherbet
4 7-ounce bottles lemon-lime
carbonated beverage, chilled

In punch bowl, combine fruit juices, water, soft drink powder, and sugar. Stir till soft drink powder and sugar are completely dissolved. Top with large spoonfuls of sherbet. Resting bottle on rim of bowl, carefully pour in carbonated beverage. Serve some sherbet with each cup. Makes 30 to 35 servings.

OLD-TIME LEMONADE

1 cup sugar
1 cup water
1 cup lemon juice
4 cups water

Combine sugar, the 1 cup water, and lemon juice. Stir till sugar is dissolved. Add remaining water. Serve over ice with mint sprigs and lemon slices. Makes 6½ cups.

CRANBERRY SPARKLE

1 1-pound can jellied
   cranberry sauce
¾ cup orange juice
¼ cup lemon juice
1 1-pint 12-ounce bottle (3½ cups)
   ginger ale, chilled

Beat cranberry sauce till smooth; stir in juices. Pour cranberry mixture over ice cubes in 2-quart pitcher or punch bowl. Resting bottle on rim, carefully pour in ginger ale. Makes 12 to 15 servings.

LEMON PUNCH

2 cups sugar
4 teaspoons grated lemon peel
1 cup lemon juice
1 to 2 pints lemon sherbet
1 to 2 pints orange sherbet
2 1-pint 12-ounce bottles
   ginger ale, chilled

Combine sugar and 2 cups water; heat, stirring constantly, till sugar dissolves; cool. Add 2 cups water, lemon peel and juice; chill. Pour into chilled punch bowl; add scoops of sherbet, stirring till partially melted. Pour ginger ale down side of bowl, stirring with an up-and-down motion. Serve *immediately* in punch cups. Makes 4 quarts.

CRANBERRY TEA PUNCH

2½ cups boiling water
 5 tea bags *or* 5 teaspoons
   loose tea
¼ teaspoon ground cinnamon
¼ teaspoon ground nutmeg
   • • •
¾ cup sugar
1 pint cranberry-juice cocktail
1½ cups water
½ cup orange juice
⅓ cup lemon juice

Pour boiling water over tea and spices. Cover and let steep 5 minutes. Remove tea bags, or strain. Add sugar; stir till dissolved; cool. Add remaining ingredients; chill. Serve over ice cubes. Makes 6 to 8 servings.

SPICED PERCOLATOR PUNCH

9 cups unsweetened pineapple juice
9 cups cranberry-juice cocktail
4½ cups water
1 cup brown sugar
   • • •
4½ teaspoons whole cloves
4 cinnamon sticks, broken in pieces
¼ teaspoon salt

Combine pineapple juice, cranberry-juice cocktail, water, and brown sugar in 30-cup automatic coffeemaker. Place cloves, cinnamon stick pieces, and salt in coffeemaker basket. Assemble coffeemaker; plug in and perk. Serve piping hot. Makes about 23 cups.

FROSTY PARTY PUNCH

2 3-ounce packages raspberry-
   flavored gelatin
1 3-ounce package cherry-flavored
   gelatin
3 cups boiling water
5 cups cold water
2 12-ounce cans (3 cups) unsweetened pineapple juice, chilled
1 12-ounce can (1½ cups) frozen
   orange juice concentrate
1 1-quart tray ice cubes
2 pints pineapple *or* lemon sherbet

Dissolve raspberry- and cherry-flavored gelatins in boiling water. Add cold water, pineapple juice, and orange juice concentrate.* Stir in ice cubes just till melted. Spoon in sherbet. Serve *immediately*. Serves 32.

*If desired, prepare this mixture several hours ahead; keep at room temperature. Just before serving, add ice and sherbet.

CIDER SNAP

In saucepan, combine 1 quart cider *or* apple juice and 2 tablespoons red cinnamon candies. Heat and stir till candies dissolve and cider is hot. Serve in mugs with apple-slice floaters. Makes 6 to 8 servings.

Orange and lime slices with maraschino →
cherry topknots trim Cranberry Sparkle.
Canned sauce gives punch a fast start.

RUBY WINE PUNCH

Sophisticated party punch makes festive fare—

- ¾ cup water
- ¾ cup sugar
- 6 inches stick cinnamon
- 1 teaspoon whole cloves
  .Dash salt
- 2 cups Burgundy
- 1 1-quart bottle cranberry-apple juice
- 1 lemon, thinly sliced

In saucepan, combine water, sugar, stick cinnamon, cloves, and salt; bring to boil. Reduce heat and simmer for 10 minutes; strain; chill syrup. Combine syrup, wine, and cranberry-apple juice. Pour over ice in punch bowl. Float lemon slices. Makes 7 cups.

Two-tone Cocktail—tomato juice, then a two-juice blend and pineapple chaser.

TWO-TONE COCKTAIL

- 4 cups chilled unsweetened pineapple juice
- 4 cups chilled tomato juice
- 4 thin lemon slices, halved

Into each 8-ounce glass, pour ½ cup pineapple juice; then tip glass and *slowly* pour ½ cup tomato juice down side of glass. Float lemon atop. Trim with watercress. Serves 8.
  Note: To fix drinks ahead of time, store in the refrigerator; use within 1 hour.

SEA FOAM PUNCH

- 1 ½-ounce envelope unsweetened lemon-lime-flavored soft drink powder
- ½ cup sugar
- 1 quart cold milk
- 1 pint vanilla ice cream
- 2 7-ounce bottles lemon-lime carbonated beverage, chilled

Place soft drink powder, sugar, and milk in large punch bowl. Stir to dissolve. Add ice cream in small spoonfuls. Resting bottle on rim of bowl, carefully pour lemon-lime beverage down side. Stir with up-and-down motion. *Serve immediately*. Makes 15 servings.

GINGER FRUIT COOLER

- 1 ½-ounce envelope unsweetened strawberry-flavored soft drink powder
- 1 cup sugar
- 4 cups cold water
- 2½ cups orange juice
- 1 cup unsweetened pineapple juice
- ½ cup lemon juice
- 1 1-pint 12-ounce bottle ginger ale, chilled

Dissolve soft drink powder and sugar in water. Add fruit juices; chill thoroughly. Just before serving, add ginger ale. Serves 12.

PINEAPPLE CITRUS PUNCH

- 1 12-ounce can (1½ cups) unsweetened pineapple juice
- 1 cup orange juice
- ¼ cup lemon juice
- 2 tablespoons honey
- 1 tablespoon maraschino cherry juice
- 1 pint vanilla ice cream
- 2 7-ounce bottles ginger ale, chilled

Mix juices, honey, and cherry juice; chill. Pour over ice in punch bowl. Add vanilla ice cream in small spoonfuls. Resting bottle on rim of bowl, carefully pour in ginger ale. *Serve immediately*. Makes 7 cups.

POPFREEZE PUNCH

What fun for kids to see fruit-flavored ice cubes become pink punch as they melt in a fizzing drink!

> 1 ½-ounce envelope unsweetened raspberry-flavored soft drink powder
> ½ cup sugar
> 4 cups unsweetened pineapple juice
> 1 1-pint 12-ounce bottle (3½ cups) lemon-lime carbonated beverage, chilled

Mix drink powder, sugar, and juice. Freeze in two ice cube trays. To serve, place cubes in glasses; fill with lemon-lime beverage; stir to blend flavors. Serves 8.

APPLE BLUSH

> 4 cups cider or apple juice
> 1 12-ounce can (1½ cups) apricot nectar
> ½ cup lemon juice
> ¼ cup grenadine syrup
> 1 1-pint 12-ounce bottle ginger ale, chilled
> 1 pint lemon sherbet

Combine juices and grenadine; chill. Pour over ice in punch bowl. Resting bottle on rim of bowl, slowly add ginger ale. Float scoops of sherbet. Makes 9½ cups.

ICED FRUIT TEA

> 3 cups boiling water
> 2 tablespoons tea leaves *or* 6 tea bags
> ½ cup sugar
>   . . .
> ½ cup orange juice
> ⅓ cup lemon juice
> 2 7-ounce bottles (about 2 cups) ginger ale, chilled

Pour boiling water over tea; cover and let stand 5 minutes; strain. Add sugar and stir till dissolved. Add fruit juices. Pour into pitcher half full of ice. Just before serving, carefully pour ginger ale down side of pitcher. Trim with mint. Makes 5½ cups.

To add carbonated beverages, rest bottle on rim of glass; pour slowly down side. Stir up-and-down.

Easy way to add spices—put spices in metal tea holder. No straining!

For melon punch bowl, cut a slice off bottom of melon to make level. Cut top third off melon. Using cup as guide, trace scallops around top edge of melon. Carve out scallops following pattern; scoop out fruit.

Fancy ice ring adds glamour to punch!
Fill ring mold half full of water and freeze in coldest part of freezer. Arrange fruit design atop; add enough water to anchor to ice. Freeze (add more water if fruit doesn't freeze to ring in 1 hour). Unmold, fruit side up.
Or freeze fruit juice, tinted water, or fruit in ice cube tray; serve in glasses.

HOT MULLED CIDER

½ cup brown sugar
1 teaspoon whole allspice
1 teaspoon whole cloves
¼ teaspoon salt
Dash ground nutmeg
3 inches stick cinnamon
2 quarts cider or apple juice

In large saucepan, combine all ingredients. Slowly bring to boil; cover and simmer 20 minutes. Strain. Serve over clove-studded orange wedges in mugs. Makes 8 servings.

SPICED WASSAIL

Traditional refreshment for the holiday season—

Break 6 inches stick cinnamon in pieces; tie in cheesecloth bag with 16 whole cloves and 1 teaspoon whole allspice. Stud 3 medium oranges with whole cloves.

In saucepan, combine 6 cups apple juice or cider, 1 pint bottle (2 cups) cranberry-juice cocktail, ¼ cup sugar, and 1 teaspoon aromatic bitters. Add spice bag and oranges; simmer, covered, 10 minutes. Stir in 1 cup rum and heat through. Remove spices and oranges. Pour into warm serving bowl and float oranges atop. Makes 9 cups.

GOLDEN WASSAIL

4 cups unsweetened pineapple juice
1 12-ounce can (1½ cups) apricot nectar
4 cups cider or apple juice
1 cup orange juice
6 inches stick cinnamon
1 teaspoon whole cloves
¼ teaspoon whole cardamom seeds, crushed

In large saucepan, combine all ingredients. Heat to boiling; reduce heat and simmer 15 to 20 minutes; strain. Pour into mugs; trim with floaters of thin orange slices studded with whole cloves. Makes 9 cups.

← Hot Mulled Cider glows with the amber beauty of a sunny fall day. Swirl slim cinnamon stick in each mug for muddler.

HOT BUTTERED LEMONADE

A comforting drink for a cold, blustery night—

½ cup sugar
3 cups boiling water
1 to 2 tablespoons butter or margarine
1 teaspoon grated lemon peel
½ cup lemon juice

Heat sugar, water, butter, and lemon peel till sugar dissolves and mixture boils. Add lemon juice. Pour into mugs and top with floaters of thin lemon slices. Makes 4 servings.

SPICY ORANGE TEA

1 cup water
10 whole cloves
1 stick cinnamon, broken
⅓ cup honey
1 cup water
1 cup orange juice
4 tea bags
Aromatic bitters

Combine 1 cup water, cloves, and cinnamon. Simmer, covered, for 10 minutes. Add honey, 1 cup water, and orange juice; bring to boiling. Remove from heat; add tea bags; let steep, covered, 5 minutes. Remove tea bags and spices. Dash in bitters to taste. Serve in cups with floaters of quartered orange slices. Makes 4 or 5 servings.

CAFE ARUBA

3 cups hot double-strength coffee
¼ cup orange peel cut in very thin strips
1 orange, peeled and sliced
1 tablespoon sugar
1 teaspoon aromatic bitters
½ cup whipping cream, whipped and sweetened to taste

Measure hot coffee into glass pot. Add orange peel and slices. Let mixture steep over low heat for about 15 minutes. Add sugar and bitters. Do not boil. Strain and pour into warmed, footed glasses. Top with sweetened whipped cream. Makes 4 or 5 servings.

Enticing appetizers

PAPAYA DELUXE

Halve lengthwise and seed 2 chilled papayas. Sprinkle with 4 teaspoons lime juice. Fill centers of papayas with 1 cup sliced fresh strawberries. Dust lightly with confectioners' sugar. Makes 4 servings.

RAINBOW MELON JULEP

Combine ¼ cup honey, 1 teaspoon shredded orange peel, ½ cup orange juice, 1 teaspoon lime peel, 2 tablespoons lime juice, and 1 tablespoon chopped fresh mint. Pour over 4 cups melon balls (watermelon, cantaloupe, and honeydew). Chill at least 2 hours. Garnish with fresh mint sprigs. Serves 4.

Frosted Grapes: Combine slightly beaten egg white and a little water; brush over clusters of grapes, then sprinkle with granulated sugar. Let dry on rack.

SUMMER FRUIT MEDLEY

2 cups sliced, peeled peaches
1 cup diced, pared pears
½ to 1 cup fresh blueberries
¼ cup lemon juice
½ cup sugar
Dash salt

Mix the fruits in a bowl. Combine remaining ingredients, stirring to dissolve sugar; pour over fruits. Toss; chill. Serves 5.

FRUIT CUP TOWER

• Melon Cocktail: Combine cantaloupe balls and watermelon scoops (use a shovel-shaped ice cream scooper). Dash melon balls with orange or cherry liqueur to taste. Chill thoroughly. Serve in sherbet dishes.
• Strawberry Starter: Rinse, hull, and halve fresh strawberries (or use frozen, unsweetened strawberries, partially thawed). Spoon into sherbet dishes. Combine one 8-ounce carton strawberry-flavored yogurt, ¼ cup sugar, and few drops red food coloring. Drizzle over berries. Garnish with mint sprigs.
• Blueberry-honeydew Cup: Combine honeydew melon balls, fresh blueberries, and finely snipped candied ginger; chill. Spoon into sherbet dishes. Resting bottle on rim of dish, slowly pour in enough chilled ginger ale to cover the bottom of the dish. Serve with lime wedges to squeeze over fruit.
• Raspberry-nectarine Cocktail: Combine raspberries, nectarine slices, and small chunks of fresh pineapple. Spoon into sherbet dishes. Garnish with sprinkling of confectioners' sugar. Tuck in a sprig of fresh mint.
• Banana-berry Cup: Peel and slice bananas; sprinkle with lemon juice. Combine with fresh blackberries and spoon into sherbet dishes. Drizzle with Orange Sour Cream Topper: Combine 1 cup dairy sour cream, ¼ cup orange juice, ½ teaspoon grated orange peel, and 2 tablespoons sugar; mix well.
• Cantaloupe Supreme: Halve and seed 2 cantaloupes. Scoop out melon balls, leaving ¼-inch shell on 3 melon halves. Drain two 10-ounce packages frozen raspberries, thawed, reserving syrup. Combine reserved syrup, 3 to 4 tablespoons cream sherry, and the melon balls. Spoon into the 3 melon shells; chill. At serving time, top melons with scoops of pineapple sherbet and drained raspberries. To serve, spoon sherbet into sauce dishes, then spoon melon balls and juice atop.
• Cantaloupe Especiale: Cut icy cold cantaloupe into wedges. Trim each with a cluster of sugar frosted seedless green grapes.

Use Fruit Cup Tower as a guide to succulent fruit combinations, then add imagination—feature fruits in season! →

CANTALOUPE MIST

    1 large ripe cantaloupe
    ¼ teaspoon ground cinnamon
    1 6-ounce can frozen orange juice
       concentrate, thawed
    2 juice cans water
    2 tablespoons lime juice

Halve and seed melon. Scoop out pulp. In blender container, combine melon pulp and cinnamon. Blend till pureed. Mix orange juice concentrate, water, and lime juice. Add melon puree mixture. Chill thoroughly. Serve in ice jacket; garnish with lime wedges or mint sprigs. Makes 6 cups.

BROILED GRAPEFRUIT

    2 large grapefruit, halved
    ¼ cup butter or margarine, melted
    ¼ cup orange liqueur
    2 teaspoons sugar

Cut around every section of grapefruit, close to membrane (fruit should be completely loosened from shell). Combine melted butter, orange liqueur, and sugar; drizzle over cut fruit. Let stand at room temperature about 2 hours to marinate fruit.

Broil grapefruit in shallow baking pan 4 inches from heat about 10 minutes or long enough to brown tops of fruit and till bubbling hot. Makes 4 servings.

CHILLED AVO-MATO SOUP

    2 avocados, pitted and peeled
    ½ cup dairy sour cream
    3 medium tomatoes, peeled and
       finely chopped (2 cups)
    1 10½-ounce can (1¼ cups) con-
       densed beef broth
    ¼ cup finely snipped green onion
    1 teaspoon salt
    1 tablespoon lemon juice
       Dash bottled hot pepper sauce

Blend avocados and sour cream with electric blender. (Or sieve avocados; mix well with sour cream.) Stir in remaining ingredients. Chill thoroughly. Trim with sour cream and snipped green onion tops. Serves 4 to 6.

CHUTNEY-CHEDDAR SPREAD

    1 4-ounce package (1 cup) shredded
       natural Cheddar cheese
    ¼ cup chopped chutney
    2 tablespoons butter or margarine
    1 teaspoon instant minced onion
    ¼ teaspoon Worcestershire sauce
       Dash bottled hot pepper sauce

Combine all ingredients in small mixing bowl. Beat with electric mixer till fluffy. Serve with assorted crackers. Makes ⅔ cup.

AVOCADO COCKTAIL SPREAD

    2 large ripe avocados, pitted,
       peeled, and slightly mashed
    1 6½-ounce can tuna, drained
    2 tablespoons lemon juice
    ½ teaspoon salt
    2 teaspoons prepared horseradish
       Dash bottled hot pepper sauce

Combine all ingredients; mix well. Cover and chill. Serve with crackers. Makes 2 cups.

DEVILED GUACAMOLE

    2 avocados, pitted and peeled
    1 teaspoon grated onion
    2 tablespoons chopped green chilies
    1 2¼-ounce can deviled ham
    2 teaspoons lemon juice

Mash avocados with fork. Stir in remaining ingredients and dash salt; chill. Serve with corn chips and crackers. Makes 1½ cups.

SASSY FRANKS

    ¼ cup plum jelly
    ¼ cup chutney, finely chopped
    1 teaspoon vinegar
       Dash garlic salt
    1 5½-ounce package cocktail
       franks (or 1 4-ounce can
       Vienna sausages, halved)

In chafing dish, mix jelly, chutney, vinegar, and garlic salt. Add franks; heat through, stirring constantly. Serve hot with picks.

Triple Treat Appetizers—meat balls, shrimp, and chicken livers complemented by sweet-sour sauce delicately flavored with pineapple.

TRIPLE TREAT APPETIZERS

- 2 tablespoons cornstarch
- 2 tablespoons sugar
- ½ teaspoon monosodium glutamate
- 1 chicken bouillon cube
- ⅓ cup vinegar
- 1 cup pineapple juice
- 2 tablespoons soy sauce
- 1 tablespoon butter or margarine
- ½ pound tiny meatballs, cooked
- ½ pound shrimp, cooked
- ½ pound chicken livers, cooked

Combine cornstarch, sugar, monosodium glutamate, and bouillon cube. Add ½ cup water, the vinegar, pineapple juice, soy, and butter. Cook and stir to boiling; cover and simmer 5 minutes. Group meatballs, shrimp, and livers in sauce. Heat through; serve hot with cocktail forks. Makes 1½ cups sauce.

CRANBERRY WIENER BITES

Zippy curry-spiked sauce coats cocktail franks—

- ¼ cup sugar
- ¾ teaspoon curry powder
- ½ teaspoon salt
- ⅛ teaspoon ground ginger
- 1 8-ounce can (1 cup) jellied cranberry sauce
- ¼ cup vinegar
- 1 tablespoon molasses
- ¾ teaspoon Worcestershire sauce
- 2 5½-ounce packages cocktail franks, halved

In saucepan, mix sugar, curry powder, salt, ginger, cranberry sauce, vinegar, molasses, and Worcestershire sauce. Bring to boil; simmer 5 minutes. Add franks and simmer 5 minutes longer. Makes 2⅓ cups.

ENTREES
AND
RELISHES

*Festive fruit garnish and
frill put Peachy
Glazed Ham in the glamour
class. A fruit accent
makes for great
flavor combinations
with meat, poultry, and fish.*

Beef eaters' specials

ORANGE POT ROAST

Combine 1½ teaspoons salt, ½ teaspoon ground cumin, ¼ teaspoon ground cloves, and ⅛ teaspoon pepper. Make small slits in one 3- to 4-pound chuck pot roast; in each cut insert some of the mixture. Melt 1 tablespoon fat in large skillet or Dutch oven. Brown meat on both sides. Add one 6-ounce can frozen orange juice concentrate, thawed, and ¾ cup water. Cover and simmer 2½ to 3 hours, or till meat is tender.

Add 1 cup bias-cut celery slices; simmer covered 10 to 12 minutes longer. Arrange one 5-ounce can bamboo shoots, drained, and one 11-ounce can mandarin oranges, drained, on top. Cook, covered, about 5 to 7 minutes. Remove meat to warm platter. Skim fat from liquid. Blend 1 tablespoon cornstarch and 2 tablespoons cold water; slowly add to liquid in pan, stirring constantly. Cook and stir till thick. Pass vegetables in serving bowl. Makes 6 to 8 servings.

FLANK STEAK TERIYAKI

    1   8½-ounce can pineapple slices
    ⅓   cup soy sauce
    2   tablespoons dry sherry
    1   tablespoon salad oil
    1   teaspoon ground ginger
    1   clove garlic, crushed
    ½   teaspoon monosodium glutamate
    4   flank steak pinwheels, 1½ inches thick

Drain pineapple reserving syrup. Combine syrup and next 6 ingredients; pour over meat and marinate 1 hour. Broil 4 to 5 inches from heat for 7 minutes, brushing once with marinade. Turn and broil 5 to 7 minutes longer, again brushing once with marinade. Add pineapple slices to broiler during last 3 or 4 minutes of cooking and brush with marinade. Serve with hot cooked rice; garnish with tomato wedges and parsley. Makes 4 servings.

← Sparkling broiled pineapple slices and fillets or "pinwheels" of flank steak go oriental in Flank Steak Teriyaki.

CRANBERRY MEAT LOAVES

    1   pound ground beef
    1   cup cooked rice
    ½   cup tomato juice
    1   slightly beaten egg
    ¼   cup minced onion
    1   tablespoon kitchen bouquet
    1½ teaspoons salt
    1   1-pound can (2 cups) whole cranberry sauce
    ⅓   cup brown sugar
    1   tablespoon lemon juice

Thoroughly combine first 7 ingredients; shape into 5 loaves. Place in 13x9x2-inch baking dish. Combine remaining ingredients; spoon over loaves. Bake at 350° for 40 minutes. Remove meat loaves to warm serving platter. Pour cranberry sauce into gravy boat; serve with meat. Makes 5 servings.

ORIENTAL CHI CHOW

    1   pound sirloin steak, 1-inch thick, cut in narrow strips
    ½   cup sliced green onions
    1   medium onion, cut in wedges
    1   5-ounce can bamboo shoots, drained
    1   5-ounce can water chestnuts, drained and sliced
    1   3-ounce can broiled sliced mushrooms, drained (½ cup)
    1   tablespoon sugar
    ½   cup condensed beef broth
    2   teaspoons cornstarch
    ¼   cup soy sauce
    1   1-pound can (2 cups) sliced peaches, drained
        Ginger Rice

Brown meat, half at a time, in 2 tablespoons hot fat. Add next 7 ingredients. Cover; simmer 5 minutes. Blend cornstarch, 1 tablespoon cold water, and soy sauce; add to meat. Cook and stir till thick. Add peaches; cover; heat through. Serve with *Ginger Rice:* Mix 2 cups hot cooked rice with ½ teaspoon ground ginger. Makes 4 or 5 servings.

Dried fruits and cider give Fruited Pot Roast
an extra special flavor. Accompany with sweet-
sour gravy, parsleyed potatoes, and corn.

FRUITED POT ROAST

12 dried apricots
12 dried prunes
 1 3- to 4-pound chuck pot roast
 1 cup cider or apple juice
 2 tablespoons sugar
¼ teaspoon ground cinnamon
¼ teaspoon ground ginger
 3 whole cloves
1½ cups sliced onions

Cover apricots and prunes with water. Soak
several hours. Meanwhile, brown pot roast on
both sides in a little hot fat; season with salt
and pepper. Combine cider, sugar, cinnamon,
ginger, and cloves; pour over meat. Add
onions. Cover; simmer 2 hours or till meat is
almost tender. Drain fruits; place atop meat
and cook 30 minutes longer. Thicken liquid
in pan for gravy. Serves 6 to 8.

PEACHY CORNED BEEF

 1 3-pound piece corned beef
 1 bay leaf
 1 1-pound 13-ounce can peach
   halves
¼ cup brown sugar
¼ cup catsup
 2 tablespoons vinegar
 2 teaspoons prepared mustard

Place corned beef in heavy saucepan; add
water to cover. Add bay leaf. Cover and
simmer 2½ to 3 hours or till tender. Cool
meat in liquid; remove. Slice across grain.
Place overlapping slices in 12x7½x2-inch
baking dish. Drain peaches reserving ¼ cup
syrup. Place peaches around meat. Combine
reserved syrup with remaining ingredients.
Pour over meat and peaches. Bake at 350° for
1 hour, basting occasionally. Serves 6.

SWEET-SOUR MEAT BALLS

Fast for a family on the run—

1 8¾-ounce can (1 cup)
   pineapple tidbits
¼ cup brown sugar
2 tablespoons cornstarch
¼ cup cider vinegar
1 teaspoon soy sauce
1 1-pound can meat balls in gravy
1 5-ounce can water chestnuts,
   drained and thinly sliced
   (⅔ cup)
1 green pepper, cut in strips
   Hot cooked rice

Drain pineapple tidbits, reserving syrup. In medium saucepan, combine brown sugar and cornstarch. Blend in pineapple syrup, ½ cup cold water, vinegar, and soy sauce. Cook and stir over low heat till mixture thickens. Carefully stir in meat balls in gravy, water chestnuts, green pepper, and pineapple tidbits. Heat to boiling. Serve over hot rice. Garnish with tomatoes if desired. Makes 4 servings.

FRUITED GROUND MEAT

1 pound ground beef
1 tablespoon salad oil
2 tablespoons chopped green onion
1 clove garlic, minced
½ cup light raisins
¼ teaspoon ground nutmeg
1¼ teaspoons salt
   Dash pepper
1 cup Burgundy
1 8¾-ounce can (1 cup)
   pineapple tidbits
1 tablespoon cornstarch
1 medium green pepper, cut in
   strips
   Hot cooked rice

Brown beef in oil in a large skillet. Add next 6 ingredients. Stir in Burgundy. Cover and simmer 10 minutes. Drain pineapple, reserving syrup. Combine cornstarch and pineapple syrup; add to meat mixture; cook and stir till mixture thickens. Add green pepper and pineapple and cook for 5 minutes or till pepper is crisp-tender. Serve over hot fluffy rice. Makes 4 servings.

APPLESAUCE MEAT LOAF

1 cup soft bread crumbs
½ cup applesauce
2 tablespoons finely chopped onion
½ teaspoon salt
   Dash pepper
1 teaspoon dried celery flakes
1 teaspoon Dijon-style mustard
1 slightly beaten egg
1 pound ground beef

   • • •

½ cup applesauce
1 tablespoon brown sugar
1 tablespoon vinegar
1 teaspoon Dijon-style mustard

Combine bread crumbs and ½ cup applesauce. Add onion, salt, pepper, celery flakes, 1 teaspoon mustard, the egg, and beef; blend thoroughly. Place in a 9x9x2-inch baking pan, shaping into round loaf. With bowl of spoon, make a depression in top of loaf.

Tangy Apple Sauce: Combine ½ cup applesauce, brown sugar, vinegar, and 1 teaspoon mustard; pour into depression in meat loaf. Bake in moderate oven (350°) for 1 hour. Makes 4 or 5 servings.

CRANBERRY POT ROAST

2 tablespoons all-purpose flour
1 teaspoon salt
1 teaspoon onion salt
¼ teaspoon pepper
1 3- to 4-pound round bone pot
   roast
2 tablespoons salad oil
4 whole cloves
2 inches stick cinnamon
¼ cup water
1 1-pound can (2 cups) whole
   cranberry sauce
1 tablespoon vinegar

Combine first 4 ingredients; rub onto surfaces of meat (use all of mixture). In Dutch oven, slowly brown meat on both sides in oil. Add spices and water. Cover tightly; simmer about 2½ hours or till tender. Add more water if necessary. Pour off excess fat. Add cranberry sauce, 2 tablespoons water, and vinegar; cover and cook 10 to 15 minutes. Pass sauce with meat. Serves 6 to 8.

Pork features

PORK WITH ORANGE SAUCE

  1 2-pound pork tenderloin
  2 tablespoons butter or margarine
  ½ cup chopped onion
  1 teaspoon grated orange peel
  ⅔ cup orange juice
  ⅓ cup dry sherry
  2 tablespoons sugar
  2 teaspoons salt
  1 medium bay leaf
  1 tablespoon cornstarch
  1 tablespoon cold water

In medium skillet, brown tenderloin on all sides in butter. Remove meat. Cook onion in same skillet till tender but not brown. Add orange peel and juice, wine, sugar, salt, bay leaf, and dash pepper. Return meat to skillet. Simmer, covered, for 1 hour or till tender, turning occasionally.

Remove meat to hot platter; slice and keep warm. Combine cornstarch and cold water; stir into pan juices and return to boiling. Cook and stir 1 to 2 minutes more. Remove bay leaf. Drizzle some sauce over meat; pass additional sauce. Makes 6 to 8 servings.

PORK CHOPS ALEXANDER

  ½ cup boiling water
 12 dried apricot halves
  6 pork chops, ¾-inch thick
  1 teaspoon salt
    Dash pepper
  ¼ teaspoon dried thyme leaves, crushed
  ¼ cup maple-flavored syrup

Pour boiling water over apricots; cool to room temperature; drain, reserving liquid. In skillet, brown chops on both sides in hot fat. Combine seasonings, maple-flavored syrup, and reserved liquid; pour over chops. Place apricots on top of chops.

Cover; cook over low heat about 1 hour or till chops are done—no pink. (Add water to sauce, if necessary, to prevent chops from sticking.) Cook uncovered last few minutes, spooning sauce over chops. Serves 6.

ORANGE CHUTNEY CHOPS

In heavy skillet, brown 4 loin pork chops (¾ inch thick) well on both sides over medium heat; pour off excess fat. Add ¼ cup water; cover and simmer till tender, about 45 minutes. Combine ½ cup chopped chutney, ¼ cup sugar, ¼ cup water, and 2 tablespoons lemon juice. Peel 1 orange and cut in four ½-inch slices. Place over chops. Pour chutney mixture over.

Continue cooking chops, spooning liquid over occasionally, for 10 to 15 minutes or till liquid becomes slightly syrupy. Arrange chops on platter. Stir pan juices and pour over chops. Makes 4 servings.

ROAST PORK TANGERINE

  1 5- to 6-pound pork loin roast
  1 teaspoon dry mustard
  1 teaspoon dried marjoram leaves, crushed
  1 teaspoon salt
  2 teaspoons grated tangerine peel
  ½ cup tangerine juice
  1 tablespoon brown sugar

      • • •

  3 tablespoons all-purpose flour
  ⅛ teaspoon dry mustard
    Pinch dried marjoram leaves, crushed
  2 tangerines, peeled and sectioned

Place pork, fat side up, on rack in shallow pan. Mix next 3 ingredients; rub over surface of meat. Roast at 325° for 2½ hours.

Skim most of fat from roasting pan. Combine tangerine peel, juice, and brown sugar; spoon over roast. Return to oven and roast 1 hour longer, or until meat thermometer registers 185°; baste frequently.

Remove meat to platter. Pour off all but about 3 tablespoons clear fat. Blend in flour, ⅛ teaspoon dry mustard, and pinch marjoram. Gradually add 1½ cups water, stirring constantly. Cook and stir till thick and bubbly. Season with salt and pepper. Just before serving, add tangerine sections to gravy. Pass with pork. Makes 10 servings.

APRICOT STUFFED CHOPS

6 to 8 double-rib pork chops
1 12-ounce can vacuum packed corn with peppers
⅓ cup fine dry bread crumbs
¼ cup chopped onion
½ teaspoon salt
½ teaspoon thyme
Dash sage

. . .

1 1-pound 14-ounce can whole apricots
1 tablespoon bottled steak sauce
1 teaspoon salt
1 teaspoon whole cloves

Cut pocket in each chop, cutting from fat side almost to bone edge. Season with salt and pepper. Combine corn, crumbs, onion, ½ teaspoon salt, thyme, and sage. Spoon stuffing lightly into chops.

Arrange chops in single layer in 13x9x2-inch baking dish. Cover tightly with foil. Bake in moderate oven (350°) for 30 minutes.

Meanwhile, drain syrup from apricots into medium saucepan; stir in steak sauce and 1 teaspoon salt. Boil, uncovered, until reduced to ½ cup. Stud apricots with cloves.

Uncover chops (do not turn) and bake 45 minutes longer. Add apricots to baking dish. Brush chops and apricots with glaze. Bake, uncovered, 25 minutes more. Garnish with parsley. Makes 6 to 8 servings.

SWEET AND SOUR CHOPS

6 pork chops, ¾ inch thick
1 1-pound can fruit cocktail
3 tablespoons vinegar
3 tablespoons brown sugar
1 tablespoon cornstarch
1 teaspoon instant minced onion
½ teaspoon salt
¼ teaspoon dried dill weed

Brown chops; pour off excess fat. Drain the fruit reserving syrup. Add remaining ingredients to syrup; pour over chops in skillet. Cook, covered, over low heat 30 minutes or till tender, turning chops once or twice. Remove meat to platter. Stir fruit into the sauce; heat to boiling. Spoon some sauce over chops; pass remainder. Serves 6.

Fruit and double-rib pork chops make a man-sized meal. Apricot Stuffed Chops are plumped with corn, crumbs, peppers, and seasonings, then brushed with apricot glaze for sparkle and flavor. Trim with clove-studded apricots and parsley fluffs. Serve the chops with a tossed salad, hot buttered rolls, and coffee.

PORK MANDARIN

1½ pounds boneless lean pork, cut in 1-inch cubes
2 tablespoons salad oil
1 cup chicken broth*
1 11-ounce can (1⅓ cups) mandarin orange sections
¼ cup corn syrup
2 tablespoons soy sauce
2 tablespoons vinegar

. . .

2 tablespoons cornstarch
1 tablespoon grated fresh ginger-root *or* 1 teaspoon ground ginger
1 small onion, thinly sliced and separated into rings
3 cups hot cooked rice

Brown meat on all sides in hot oil. Add the broth; cover; simmer 1 hour or till tender. Drain oranges, reserving syrup. Combine reserved orange syrup, corn syrup, soy sauce, and vinegar. Blend in cornstarch and ginger. Add sauce to meat with onion rings; cook and stir till the mixture thickens. Add oranges; heat through. Serve on bed of hot cooked rice. Makes 4 or 5 servings.

*Or use 1 chicken bouillon cube dissolved in 1 cup boiling water.

ISLAND SWEET-SOUR PORK

1½ pounds boneless pork shoulder, cut in small cubes
1 tablespoon salad oil
1 teaspoon salt
1 8¾-ounce can pineapple tidbits
½ cup bottled barbecue sauce
1 tablespoon cornstarch
1 medium green pepper, cut in strips
Hot cooked rice

In skillet, brown meat in hot oil. Season with salt and dash pepper. Drain pineapple, reserving syrup. Add water to syrup to make ¾ cup. Stir syrup and barbecue sauce into browned meat. Cover and simmer 40 to 45 minutes or till tender. Blend cornstarch with 2 tablespoons cold water; stir into meat. Cook and stir till thickened. Add pineapple and green pepper; heat through. Serve over rice. Makes 6 servings.

APPLE-STUFFED PORK

2 1-pound whole pork tenderloins
Apple Stuffing
1 cup apple juice
4 slices bacon, halved

Cut each tenderloin lengthwise, *not quite through;* flatten out. Sprinkle generously with salt and pepper. Spread Apple Stuffing over one flattened loin; top with second one; skewer shut. Place in shallow baking pan. Pour 1 cup apple juice over meat and lay bacon on top. Roast uncovered at 350° for 1½ hours or till well done. Remove skewers. Make gravy from drippings. Serves 6 to 8.

Apple Stuffing: Heat ⅓ cup apple juice with 1 tablespoon butter and 1 teaspoon sage. Stir in ¾ cup chopped unpared tart apple, ½ cup chopped onion, and ¾ cup packaged herb-seasoned stuffing mix.

RIBS AND KRAUT

1 1-pound 11-ounce can (3½ cups) sauerkraut, drained
2 unpared tart apples, sliced
2 tablespoons sugar
2 to 3 teaspoons caraway seed
3 to 4 pounds loin back ribs or spareribs, cut in serving pieces
2 teaspoons salt
¼ teaspoon pepper

In Dutch oven, mix kraut, apples, sugar, and caraway seed. Season ribs with the salt and pepper; place meaty side up over kraut. Bake covered at 300° for 4 to 5 hours. Serve ribs and kraut with juices. Serves 4 to 6.

APPLE-SAUCED PORK

Place on rack in an open pan one 2-pound smoked pork shoulder roll. Roast in slow oven (325°) about 30 minutes. Meanwhile, combine one 1-pound can (2 cups) applesauce, ¼ cup brown sugar, and ¼ teaspoon *each* ground cinnamon and ground cloves.

Spread the roast with about *half* the applesauce mixture. Continue baking 1 to 1¼ hours or till meat thermometer registers 170°. Heat remaining applesauce mixture; pass with meat. Serves 6.

Zesty orange marmalade, laced with ginger and soy, bastes Spareribs Cantonese. Buttered snow peas and fluffy rice complete the meal.

SPARERIBS CANTONESE

4 pounds spareribs, cut in serving pieces
½ cup soy sauce
1 cup orange marmalade
½ teaspoon garlic powder
½ teaspoon ground ginger
Dash pepper

In a shallow roasting pan, place ribs meaty side down. Roast at 450° for 30 minutes. Remove meat from oven; drain excess fat from ribs. Turn ribs meaty side up. Lower oven temperature to 350°; continue roasting ribs for 1 hour. Combine in a small bowl, soy sauce, ¾ cup water, orange marmalade, garlic powder, ginger, and pepper; blend thoroughly. Pour over the ribs; roast for 30 minutes longer or till tender, basting ribs occasionally with the sauce. Serves 6.

SPICY ORANGE GLAZE

Blend one 6-ounce can frozen orange juice concentrate, thawed, ¼ cup prepared mustard, and ¼ cup sugar. Stir in 1 tablespoon soy sauce, 1 tablespoon dry sherry, and ½ teaspoon ginger. Baste spareribs with glaze every 15 minutes during last 1½ hours of baking time. (Prepare ribs as in Spareribs Cantonese; omit sauce.) Makes 1⅓ cups.

MEDITERRANEAN SAUCE

Combine in a saucepan, ¼ cup brown sugar and 1 tablespoon cornstarch. Blend in ⅛ teaspoon salt, ⅛ teaspoon ground cloves, 1 cup orange juice, and 2 tablespoons lemon juice. Bring to boil, stirring constantly. Add ½ cup chopped dried figs; cover and simmer 5 minutes. Serve hot with pork. Makes 1½ cups.

Ham medleys

HAM BAKED IN CIDER

1 large, fully cooked ham
4 cups cider or apple juice
2 medium onions, quartered
1 tablespoon brown sugar
1 tablespoon lemon juice
½ cup maple-flavored syrup

Place ham, fat side up, on rack in shallow pan. Score in diamonds; stud with whole cloves. Bring cider, onions, sugar, and lemon juice to boil. Cover; simmer 10 minutes. Strain; pour over ham. Heat ham following chart; baste often with cider mixture. During last 15 minutes, brush twice with maple syrup.

PINEAPPLE-ORANGE HAM

Bake a large ham according to time on chart. Meanwhile, pour ½ cup hot cider or hot water over ¼ cup raisins; let stand. Half hour before end of baking time, score fat in diamonds. Spoon Pineapple-orange Glaze over ham. Return to oven for 30 minutes; baste with glaze 2 or 3 times. Remove ham to platter. Drain raisins; add to glaze remaining in pan; heat. Pass with ham.

Pineapple-orange Glaze: Combine one 6-ounce can frozen pineapple-orange juice concentrate, thawed, ½ cup light corn syrup, ½ teaspoon ground cinnamon, and ¼ teaspoon ground cloves; bring to boiling.

TIMETABLE FOR BAKED HAM

Kind of Ham	Weight	Total Oven Time (325° Oven)	
		Fully Cooked	Cook-Before-Eating
Whole Ham, Bone-in or Semi-boneless	8 to 12 pounds 14 to 18 pounds	2¼ to 2¾ hours 3 to 3½ hours	2¾ to 3¼ hours 3½ to 4 hours
Half Ham, Bone-in	6 to 8 pounds	2 to 2¼ hours	2 to 2½ hours
Center-cut Slice, Bone-in, 2 inches thick	2½ to 3 pounds	1¼ to 1½ hours	1½ hours
Whole Ham, Boneless	8 to 10 pounds	2 to 2¼ hours	
Half Ham, Boneless	4 to 5 pounds	1½ hours	

HAM WITH CHERRY SAUCE

Heat a large canned ham according to time on can. Half hour before end of heating time, remove ham and score fat in diamonds. Combine one 10-ounce jar apple *or* guava jelly and 1 tablespoon prepared mustard; stir in ⅓ cup unsweetened pineapple juice and 2 tablespoons dry white wine. Cook and stir to boiling; simmer 3 minutes. Pour ⅓ of glaze over ham; return to oven for 30 minutes. Spoon on glaze every 10 minutes.

In saucepan, heat one 1-pound 5-ounce can cherry pie filling and ½ cup light raisins to boiling; stir occasionally. Remove ham to platter. Add glaze from pan to cherry sauce. Bring to boil. Spoon some over ham. Pass remainder. Makes 3 cups sauce.

TO SCORE AND GLAZE HAM

Half hour before heating or cooking time is up, remove ham from oven and pour fat drippings from pan. Score ham fat in diamonds—the cuts should be only ¼ inch deep. A strip of heavy paper, 12x2 inches, makes an easy guide for cutting parallel lines. Stud ham with whole cloves at points where scoring lines cross, if desired.

After scoring, spoon glaze, if used, over ham. Return to slow oven (325°) for 30 minutes. For a heavy glaze, baste ham several times during last half hour of heating.

An apple-pineapple glaze sparks Ham → with Cherry Sauce. The sauce is a quickie —canned cherry pie filling and raisins.

CRANBERRY GLAZED HAM

1 2-pound ham slice,
1½ inches thick
½ cup brown sugar
2 tablespoons cornstarch
Dash ground cloves
Dash salt
1½ cups cranberry-juice cocktail
½ cup orange juice
½ cup raisins

Slash fat edge of ham at 2-inch intervals. Insert whole cloves in fat, if desired. Place ham in shallow baking dish. Bake in a slow oven (325°) for 30 minutes.

Meanwhile, make *Cranberry Sauce:* Mix brown sugar, cornstarch, cloves, and salt. Add fruit juices and raisins. Cook and stir till mixture thickens and boils. Spoon part of sauce over ham; bake 20 minutes more or till glazed. Pass remaining sauce. Serves 6.

SPICED FRUIT SAUCE

1 8¾-ounce can pineapple tidbits
1 8¾-ounce can apricot halves
3 inches stick cinnamon
12 whole cloves
2 tablespoons sugar
2 teaspoons cornstarch
½ cup raisins

Drain pineapple and apricots, reserving syrups. Cut apricots in quarters. Combine syrups and spices; cover and simmer 5 minutes. Remove spices. Combine sugar and cornstarch; stir in small amount of hot syrup, mixing well; return to hot mixture. Cook, stirring constantly, till mixture thickens and boils. Add apricots, pineapple, and raisins; cook 5 minutes; stir occasionally. If desired, add aromatic bitters to taste. Serve warm over a heated ham slice. Makes 1¾ cups sauce.

CURRANT GLAZE

Melt ½ cup currant jelly, stirring till smooth. Add 1 tablespoon vinegar, ½ teaspoon dry mustard, ¼ teaspoon ground cinnamon, and dash ground cloves. Brush ham with glaze occasionally during last 30 minutes of heating time and before serving.

PEACHY GLAZED HAM

Cook a ham according to time on chart. Half an hour before cooking time is up, pour off drippings. Score ham and stud with whole cloves. Spoon Glaze over ham. Cook 30 minutes more, spooning Glaze over 2 or 3 times. Remove to platter. Add paper frill. Arrange peaches and oranges (from Sauce) atop ham; anchor with whole cloves or small picks.

Spicy Peach Sauce: In saucepan, combine one 1-pound 13-ounce can sliced peaches (with syrup), ⅓ cup vinegar, ¾ cup sugar, 1 teaspoon whole cloves, 6 inches stick cinnamon, and 10 whole allspice. Cut 1 unpeeled orange into wedges; add. Heat to boiling; simmer, uncovered, 5 minutes. Cover; cool. Remove spices. Serve sauce warm or chilled.

Glaze: Drain 1 cup syrup from Spicy Peach Sauce; boil gently, uncovered, till reduced by half, about 15 minutes.

BURGUNDY HAM

1 tablespoon butter or margarine
2 tablespoons sugar
Dash ground ginger
1 2¼-pound ham slice, 1½ inches thick
¾ cup Burgundy *or* port
1 tablespoon cornstarch
1 cup seedless green grapes

Melt butter in skillet. Sprinkle in sugar and ginger. Brown ham quickly in mixture. Remove ham. Blend wine into sugar mixture; cook and stir till boiling. Combine cornstarch and ¼ cup cold water. Add to wine mixture. Cook and stir till mixture thickens and boils. Return ham to skillet; cover; simmer 15 minutes. Add grapes; cook 1 to 2 minutes. Spoon sauce over ham on platter. Serves 6.

CURRANT-RAISIN SAUCE

Combine ⅓ cup raisins, ½ cup water, ⅓ cup currant jelly, ½ teaspoon grated orange peel, and ½ cup orange juice in saucepan; bring to boil. Combine 2 tablespoons brown sugar, 1 tablespoon cornstarch, dash *each* ground allspice and salt; stir into orange mixture. Cook and stir till thick and clear. Serve warm over cooked ham slice.

HAWAIIAN HAM SUPPER

2 cups cooked ham cut in julienne strips
2 tablespoons shortening
1 8¾-ounce can pineapple tidbits
3 tablespoons brown sugar
3 tablespoons cornstarch
2 tablespoons prepared mustard
2 tablespoons vinegar
Dash pepper
¾ cup coarsely chopped green pepper
Hot cooked rice

Lightly brown ham in shortening in large skillet. Drain pineapple, reserving syrup. Combine syrup, 1½ cups water, sugar, cornstarch, mustard, vinegar, and pepper. Add to ham mixture; cook and stir till thickened. Add green pepper and pineapple; heat to boiling. Cook and stir 1 to 2 minutes more. Serve over fluffy hot rice. Serves 4 to 6.

HAM PINEAPPLE LOAF

Thoroughly combine 1 pound ground cooked ham, ½ pound ground fresh pork, ½ cup coarse saltine cracker crumbs (about 8 crackers), ¼ cup chopped onion, ¼ cup milk, 1 egg, 1 tablespoon snipped parsley, and dash pepper. Shape mixture into 6 patties, matching diameter to large pineapple slices. (You'll need 6 slices; reserve syrup.)

In 12x7½x2-inch baking dish, line up a row of alternating ham patties and pineapple slices; insert a skewer (at least 2 inches longer than the loaf) through patties and pineapple slices. Bake in slow oven (325°) for 30 minutes.

Combine 1 cup brown sugar, ¼ cup pineapple syrup, 1 tablespoon vinegar, and 1 teaspoon prepared mustard. Pour a little of the glaze over roll; bake 30 minutes more, basting frequently with remaining glaze. Remove from baking dish to warm platter. Remove skewer. Makes 6 servings.

The tropical flavor of pineapple gives an old favorite—ham loaf—a new look and delicious flavor in company-special Ham Pineapple Loaf.

MARMALADE HAM SQUARES

1½ cups packaged herb-seasoned
    stuffing
2 cups milk
1½ pounds ground fresh pork
1½ pounds ground cooked ham
½ cup chopped onion
¼ teaspoon salt
1 cup orange marmalade
2 tablespoons vinegar
1 teaspoon dry mustard
¼ teaspoon ground cinnamon
¼ teaspoon ground cloves

Soak stuffing in milk 5 minutes; add meats, onion, and salt; mix well. Lightly pack into 9x9x2-inch baking dish. Bake in moderate oven (350°) 1¼ hours. Spoon off drippings. For marmalade glaze, mix remaining ingredients; spread over loaf. Bake 10 minutes longer. Allow to stand a few minutes before cutting in squares. Trim with orange sections. Makes 9 to 12 servings.

RAISIN HAM LOGS

1 pound ground cooked ham
½ pound ground fresh pork
¾ cup milk
½ cup quick-cooking rolled oats
1 egg
2 teaspoons prepared horseradish
½ teaspoon salt
    Dash freshly ground pepper
1 tablespoon cornstarch
¾ cup cold water
2 tablespoons lemon juice
2 tablespoons vinegar
½ cup brown sugar
¼ cup raisins

Combine first 8 ingredients; mix well. Shape into 6 logs, about 6½-inches long. Place in 11x7x1½-inch baking dish.

Blend cornstarch and water; add remaining ingredients. Cook and stir till mixture bubbles; pour over ham logs. Bake in moderate oven (350°) for 40 to 45 minutes, basting occasionally with the sauce. Makes 6 servings.

← Orange-glazed Ham Loaf stars in a tasty oven meal. Creamy scalloped potatoes and herbed carrots can bake alongside.

ORANGE-GLAZED HAM LOAF

Combine 1½ pounds ground cooked ham, 1 pound ground fresh pork, 1 cup medium cracker crumbs, 1 cup milk, ½ cup chopped onion, and 2 slightly beaten eggs. Pack lightly into loaf pan; unmold into shallow baking pan. Bake in moderate oven (350°) for 1 hour.

Combine one 6-ounce can frozen orange juice concentrate, thawed, ¼ cup prepared mustard, and ¼ cup brown sugar. Spoon over ham and bake 30 minutes, spooning glaze over several times. Last 5 minutes of cooking, top with orange sections and spoon glaze over. Pass extra glaze. Serves 8 to 10.

APRICOT HAM PATTIES

1½ pounds ground cooked ham
½ cup soft bread crumbs
½ cup milk
2 eggs
¼ cup chopped onion
1 ounce blue cheese, crumbled
    (¼ cup)
1 tablespoon Worcestershire sauce
1 teaspoon prepared mustard
¼ teaspoon sage
¼ teaspoon pepper
½ cup apricot *or* peach preserves
2 teaspoons vinegar
1 teaspoon prepared mustard

Combine ham, bread crumbs, milk, eggs, onion, cheese, Worcestershire sauce, mustard, sage, and pepper. Shape in 6 patties. Place in 13x9x2-inch baking dish; bake at 350° for 30 minutes. Combine remaining ingredients; brush on patties. Bake 10 minutes. Serves 6.

GLAZED HAM BALLS

Combine 1 pound ground cooked ham, ½ pound ground fresh pork, ¾ cup soft bread crumbs, 2 slightly beaten eggs, ½ cup milk, and 2 tablespoons chopped onion. Shape in 1½-inch balls; place in shallow baking pan.

Mix one 8¾-ounce can (1 cup) crushed pineapple, ⅓ cup brown sugar, 1 tablespoon vinegar, and 2 to 3 tablespoons prepared mustard; spoon over ham balls. Bake in moderate oven (350°) for 45 to 50 minutes, basting occasionally with glaze. Serves 6 to 8.

SPICY HAM LOAF

1 1-pound 13-ounce jar (3½ cups)
  spiced peach halves
1 pound ground cooked ham
1 pound ground fresh pork
1 cup soft bread crumbs
2 eggs
3 tablespoons chili sauce
2 tablespoons vinegar
1 teaspoon dry mustard
  Whole cloves and brown sugar

Drain peach halves reserving ½ cup syrup; arrange cut side up in bottom of 9x5x3-inch loaf pan. Combine reserved syrup with next 7 ingredients; mix well; press over peaches. Bake at 350° for 1¼ to 1½ hours. Drain off excess juices; invert on serving platter. Stud peaches with whole cloves; sprinkle with brown sugar. Bake 5 minutes. Serves 6 to 8.

FRANK AND BEAN BAKE

¼ cup chopped onion
1 tablespoon butter or margarine
2 1-pound cans (4 cups) pork and
  beans in tomato sauce
¼ cup catsup
1 tablespoon prepared mustard
1 pound (8 to 10) frankfurters
3 pineapple slices, cut in half
1 tablespoon pineapple syrup
¼ cup brown sugar
1 tablespoon prepared mustard

Cook onion in butter till tender. Add beans, catsup, and mustard; bring to boil; pour into 11x7x1½-inch baking dish. Arrange frankfurters and pineapple half-slices atop. Blend remaining ingredients; spread over franks and pineapple. Bake at 375° for 20 minutes or till hot. Makes 4 or 5 servings.

BANANAS IN HAM BLANKETS

Peel 6 large green-tipped bananas. Dash with salt, pepper, and paprika. Roll each in a thin slice of boiled ham; place in shallow baking dish. Pour 1 cup whipping cream over top; sprinkle with ¼ cup grated Parmesan cheese; dot with 2 tablespoons butter. Bake at 400° for 20 minutes. Serves 6.

SOUTHERN LUNCHEON BAKE

Each stack-up is a meal-in-one. Easy to serve!

6 slices fully cooked boneless rolled
  ham, ½ inch thick
  Whole cloves
6 canned pineapple slices
2 tablespoons butter or margarine,
  melted
½ teaspoon salt
2 cups mashed cooked or canned
  sweet potatoes
1 cup whole cranberry sauce
1 teaspoon grated orange peel
½ cup orange juice
2 tablespoons brown sugar

Stud sides of ham slices with cloves; arrange in 13x9x2-inch baking dish; top each with pineapple ring. Beat butter and salt into potatoes; mound atop pineapple. In saucepan, combine cranberry sauce, orange peel, juice, and brown sugar; simmer about 5 minutes, stirring frequently; drizzle over potatoes. Bake in moderate oven (350°) 40 to 45 minutes, basting once or twice with sauce. Serves 6.

ISLAND FRANKS

1 8¾-ounce can pineapple tidbits
2 tablespoons butter or margarine
½ cup sliced onion
1 green pepper, cut in strips
  (about 1 cup)
1 beef bouillon cube
⅓ cup boiling water
1 tablespoon cornstarch
1 tablespoon brown sugar
2 tablespoons vinegar
1 tablespoon soy sauce
½ pound (4 or 5) frankfurters,
  sliced

Drain pineapple, reserving syrup. In skillet, melt butter; add onion and green pepper; cover and cook over low heat till tender-crisp, about 5 minutes. Dissolve bouillon cube in boiling water. Combine cornstarch with brown sugar, vinegar, soy sauce, and reserved syrup; add bouillon; pour over cooked onion and pepper. Cook and stir till mixture thickens. Add franks and pineapple. Heat through. Serve over hot fluffy rice. Makes 4 servings.

All-time favorite baked beans, peaches, and luncheon meat team up in Ginger Peachy Casserole. Gingersnap crumbs add peppy twist.

GINGER PEACHY CASSEROLE

2 1-pound cans (4 cups) pork and
  beans in tomato sauce
8 gingersnaps, finely crushed
  (½ cup)
¼ cup catsup
2 tablespoons light molasses
½ teaspoon salt

· · ·

1 1-pound can peach slices, drained
1 12-ounce can luncheon meat

Combine beans, gingersnap crumbs, catsup, molasses, and salt. Place *half* the bean mixture in bottom of 2-quart casserole. Arrange peach slices over beans; top with remaining bean mixture. Cut luncheon meat in 6 slices; place atop beans. Cover and bake in slow oven (325°) for 45 minutes. Uncover and bake 15 minutes more. Makes 4 to 6 servings.

HAWAIIAN HAM PIE

1 pound ground cooked ham
⅓ cup fine dry bread crumbs
1 beaten egg
½ cup milk
1 tablespoon prepared mustard
2 tablespoons sliced green onion
1 1-pound 4½-ounce can crushed
  pineapple, well drained (1½ cups)

· · ·

1 unbaked 9-inch pastry shell

· · ·

¼ cup brown sugar

Thoroughly combine ham, crumbs, egg, milk, mustard, onion, and ½ *cup* of the pineapple. Spread in pastry shell. Combine remaining pineapple and brown sugar; arrange on ham mixture in a spoke pattern. Bake in moderate oven (350°) for 45 minutes. Serves 6 to 8.

Lamb favorites

LEG OF LAMB WEST INDIES

    1 5- to 6-pound leg of lamb
    1 clove garlic, sliced
    1 teaspoon ground ginger
    1 teaspoon dry mustard
    ½ cup cherry jam
    1 cup hot strong coffee
    2 tablespoons port

Without removing fell (thin paper-like covering), make 2 or 3 slits in leg of lamb and insert garlic. Combine ginger and mustard; rub over lamb. Place fat side up on rack in shallow roasting pan. Insert meat thermometer so tip reaches center of largest muscle. (Tip should not rest in fat or on bone.) Roast in slow oven (325°) for 3 to 3½ hours or till meat thermometer registers 175° to 180°.

After first hour of roasting, dissolve jam in coffee; stir in wine. Pour over lamb. Baste occasionally during remainder of roasting time. Lift meat to warm platter.

Pour pan juices into 2-cup measure and skim off fat; return 2 tablespoons fat to pan. Blend in 2 tablespoons flour. Add water to meat juices to make 1½ cups; stir into pan. Cook and stir till bubbly and thickened. Season to taste. Pass with lamb. Serves 10.

ORANGE-THYME LAMB

    6 lamb shoulder chops, ¾ inch thick
    ½ teaspoon shredded orange peel
    ¼ cup orange juice
    ¾ teaspoon thyme, crushed
      Dash *each* salt and pepper
    1 3-ounce can broiled sliced
      mushrooms, drained (½ cup)

Trim excess fat from chops. Combine orange peel, orange juice, and thyme; pour over the chops and marinate 1 hour at room temperature or several hours in the refrigerator. Drain, reserving the marinade.

Brown chops in small amount of fat; season with salt and pepper. Add reserved marinade and the mushrooms. Cover and simmer for 40 to 45 minutes or till tender. Uncover last few minutes of cooking. Makes 6 servings.

LAMB KABOBS

    1 1-pound 1-ounce jar purple plums
    ¼ cup lemon juice
    1 tablespoon soy sauce
    1 teaspoon Worcestershire sauce
    ½ clove garlic, crushed
    ½ teaspoon basil, crushed
    1 pound boneless lamb, cut in
      1-inch cubes
    ½ teaspoon salt

Drain plums, reserving ¼ cup syrup. Pit and sieve plums. Combine ¼ cup syrup, plums, lemon juice, soy sauce, Worcestershire sauce, garlic, and basil. Marinate lamb in plum mixture several hours. Place meat on skewers; season with salt and dash pepper. Broil 4 inches from heat 10 to 12 minutes or till done; turn and baste often. Simmer remaining marinade 5 minutes; pass with meat. Serves 4.

LAMB ROLL-UPS

    12 large romaine leaves
     1 pound ground lamb
     ½ cup chopped onion
     ½ cup raisins
     ½ cup milk
     ⅓ cup packaged precooked rice
     ¾ teaspoon salt
     1 cup condensed beef broth
     2 tablespoons lemon juice
     1 tablespoon cornstarch
     1 egg

Soften romaine leaves by crushing rib with thumb, then dipping in boiling water. Combine next 6 ingredients. Place 3 tablespoons meat mixture on each romaine leaf. Roll up, tucking in sides; secure with toothpicks. Place in skillet; pour ½ *cup* of the beef broth over. Cover; simmer 25 minutes. Add lemon juice; simmer 5 minutes. Remove roll-ups.

Combine cornstarch and remaining broth; stir into liquid in skillet. Cook and stir to boiling. Beat egg till thick and lemon-colored. Gradually stir hot sauce into egg; return to skillet; cook and stir over low heat till hot. Serve over roll-ups. Serves 6.

Sweet-sour Lamb Chops simmer in a flavorful sauce spiked with ginger. Orange slices and lemon wedges add the colorful, tangy accent.

SWEET-SOUR LAMB CHOPS

Ordinary shoulder chops go Polynesian—

Brown 4 lamb shoulder chops (about 1 inch thick) on both sides over low heat. Combine ¼ cup vinegar, ¼ cup brown sugar, 1 teaspoon salt, ½ teaspoon ground ginger, and dash pepper; pour over meat.

Top each chop with an orange slice and lemon wedge. Cover and cook over low heat for about 30 minutes or till chops are tender. Remove lamb chops to warm serving platter.

Pour pan juices into measuring cup; skim off fat; add water to pan juices to make 1 cup. Return the liquid to skillet. Blend 1 tablespoon cornstarch with 1 tablespoon cold water; stir into liquid in skillet. Cook, stirring constantly, till mixture thickens and boils. Serve sauce over lamb chops on bed of hot fluffy rice. Makes 4 servings.

ROAST STUFFED LAMB

1 4- to 5-pound lamb shoulder roast
1 cup chopped celery
¼ cup chopped onion
¼ cup butter or margarine

• • •

6 cups soft bread crumbs (8 slices)
½ cup apricot nectar
2 beaten eggs
1 teaspoon salt
2 teaspoons poultry seasoning

Have meatman bone roast to form pocket. Cook celery and onion in butter till tender. Toss with remaining ingredients. Fill pocket with stuffing; skewer securely. Place roast on rack in shallow pan. Bake in slow oven (325°) till meat thermometer registers 175° to 180° (about 3 to 3¾ hours). Remove strings and skewers before serving. Makes 8 servings.

Fruit-dressed poultry

ROAST CHICKEN ELEGANTE

- 1 3-ounce can (⅔ cup) broiled sliced mushrooms
- 1 6-ounce package long-grain and wild rice mix
- 1 tablespoon instant minced onion
- 1 14-ounce can (1¾ cups) chicken broth
- 2 3-pound whole broiler-fryer chickens
- ½ cup light corn syrup
- 2 tablespoons thinly slivered orange peel
- ¼ cup orange juice
- ½ teaspoon monosodium glutamate
- ¼ teaspoon ground ginger
- 1 orange, cut in thick slices
  Cranberry-orange relish

Drain mushrooms, reserving liquid. In medium saucepan, combine rice mix and onion; stir in chicken broth and the reserved mushroom liquid. Cook according to package directions. Stir in mushrooms. Lightly stuff chickens with rice mixture; skewer shut.

Tie drumsticks to tail. Place birds, breast side up, on rack in shallow baking pan; tuck wings under or tie across back. Roast in moderate oven (375°) for 1½ hours.

Meanwhile, combine corn syrup, orange peel, orange juice, monosodium glutamate, and ginger. Brush chickens with glaze and roast 15 minutes longer. Remove cord and skewers; let chickens stand on warm serving platter a few minutes before carving.

For garnish, cook thick orange slices in butter till warm; then top with cranberry-orange relish. Serves 8 to 10.

Roast Chicken Elegante is glazed to golden perfection with a gingery orange sauce. The superbly seasoned rice stuffing cooks inside.

CHICKEN AND CHERRIES

Tender chicken complemented with wine—

- ⅓ cup all-purpose flour
- 1½ teaspoons salt
- ½ teaspoon paprika
- ¼ teaspoon garlic salt
- 3 large chicken breasts, cut in half lengthwise
- ¼ cup butter or margarine
- 1 1-pound can (2 cups) pitted dark sweet cherries, drained
- 1 cup sauterne

Combine flour, salt, paprika, and garlic salt in paper bag; add 2 or 3 pieces of chicken at a time and shake. Melt butter in large skillet. Add chicken and brown slowly, turning once. Add cherries; pour sauterne over all. Cover and simmer about 35 minutes or till tender. Pass extra sauce. Makes 6 servings.

CHICKEN-CHOW BAKE

Chow mein noodles and soy lend an oriental touch—

- 2 cups diced cooked or canned chicken
- 1 10½-ounce can condensed cream of mushroom soup
- 1 8¾-ounce can (1 cup) pineapple tidbits
- 1 tablespoon soy sauce
- 1 cup celery slices
- 2 tablespoons snipped green onions
- 1 3-ounce can (2½ cups) chow mein noodles

Combine all ingredients except noodles, mixing well. Gently fold in *1 cup of the noodles.* Turn into 8x8x2-inch baking dish. Sprinkle with remaining noodles. Bake in moderate oven (350°) 50 minutes or till hot. Pass soy sauce. Makes 4 or 5 servings.

Serve roast chicken in grand style. Garnish the serving platter with orange slices topped with cranberry-orange relish and fluffs of parsley.

CURRANT-ORANGE CHICKEN

½ cup currant jelly
¼ cup frozen orange juice
   concentrate, thawed
2 teaspoons cornstarch
1 teaspoon dry mustard
   Dash bottled hot pepper sauce
½ cup all-purpose flour
1 teaspoon salt
1 2½- to 3-pound ready-to-cook
   broiler-fryer chicken, cut up

. . .

1 cup chopped celery
¼ cup chopped onion
¼ cup butter or margarine
2 tablespoons frozen orange juice
   concentrate, thawed
½ teaspoon salt
1⅓ cups packaged precooked rice

In a saucepan, combine jelly, ¼ cup orange juice concentrate, and ⅓ cup water; cook and stir till smooth. Blend cornstarch, dry mustard, and bottled hot pepper sauce with 1 tablespoon cold water; stir into jelly mixture; cook and stir till mixture thickens; set aside.

Combine flour and 1 teaspoon salt in paper bag. Add 2 or 3 pieces of chicken at a time; shake to coat. Brown in hot fat over medium heat, turning occasionally. Drain excess fat; add the currant-orange sauce. Cover; simmer over very low heat 45 minutes or till tender; baste occasionally with sauce.

Serve with *Orange Rice:* Cook celery and onion in butter till tender. Add 2 tablespoons orange juice concentrate, 1¼ cups water, and ½ teaspoon salt; bring to boil. Add rice; continue cooking as directed on package. Serves 4.

CHICKEN VERONIQUE

Cut one 2½- to 3-pound ready-to-cook broiler-fryer chicken in pieces. Halve a lemon; rub chicken with the cut side; sprinkle with salt. Let dry on rack 15 minutes.

Heat ⅓ cup butter in a skillet till bubbly. Brown chicken in butter (about 10 minutes), turning with tongs. Pour in ⅓ cup cooking sauterne; spoon sauce over chicken. Cover; simmer till chicken is tender (30 to 35 minutes). About 3 minutes before end of cooking, add 1 cup seedless green grapes. Dash with paprika. Pass sauce. Serves 3 or 4.

TURKEY HAWAIIAN

½ cup chopped onion
2 tablespoons butter or margarine
1 10-ounce package frozen peas
1½ cups diagonally sliced celery
1 3-ounce can (⅔ cup) broiled
   sliced mushrooms
2 chicken bouillon cubes
1 tablespoon cornstarch
1 tablespoon soy sauce
1 13½-ounce can pineapple
   tidbits, drained (1 cup)
1 5-ounce can water chestnuts,
   drained and sliced
2 cups diced cooked turkey
½ cup toasted slivered almonds

Cook onion in butter till tender. Stir in peas, celery, mushrooms, bouillon cubes, and 1 cup water; bring to boil; cover; simmer 5 minutes. Combine cornstarch and soy sauce; stir into mixture. Cook and stir till mixture boils. Add pineapple, water chestnuts, and turkey; heat through. Serve on hot rice; top with almonds. Pass soy sauce. Serves 5 or 6.

CHICKEN CURRY

1 tablespoon curry powder
1 cup finely chopped pared apple
1 tablespoon butter or margarine
½ cup finely chopped onion
1 cup sliced celery
½ cup sliced fresh *or* 1 3-ounce can
   broiled sliced mushrooms, drained
½ cup condensed beef broth
2 tablespoons cornstarch
2 tablespoons cold water
1 cup light cream
1 cup milk
2 cups diced cooked chicken
1 teaspoon salt
1 teaspoon monosodium glutamate

Cook curry powder and apple in butter till apple is soft; stir in onion, celery, and mushrooms. Add beef broth; bring to boil. Combine cornstarch and water; add, with cream and milk, to the first mixture. Cook and stir till mixture thickens. Stir in chicken, salt, and monosodium glutamate. Serve with hot rice. Offer condiments of chutney, coconut, and raisins. Makes 5 or 6 servings.

CRANBERRY DUCKLING

    2 3½- to 4-pound ready-to-cook
       ducklings
    1 10½-ounce can condensed beef
       broth (about 1¼ cups)
    ¾ cup cranberry-juice cocktail
    2 tablespoons butter or margarine
    2 tablespoons sugar
    2 tablespoons vinegar
          • • •
    1 tablespoon cornstarch
    1 tablespoon cranberry-juice
       cocktail

Place ducklings, breast side up, on rack in
shallow pan. Roast, uncovered, at 375° for
1½ hours. Raise oven temperature to 425°
and roast for 15 minutes more or till tender.

Meanwhile, place neck and giblets in saucepan. Add beef broth and simmer, covered, for
1 hour. Strain broth; serve giblets with duck.
To strained broth, add the ¾ cup cranberry-
juice cocktail; cook till reduced to 1 cup.

In small pan, melt butter; blend in sugar;
cook and stir till brown. Add vinegar and the
cranberry-broth mixture.

Remove ducklings from pan to warm serving platter. Skim fat from juices; add juices to
cranberry-broth mixture. Blend cornstarch
with the 1 tablespoon cranberry-juice cocktail; stir into sauce. Cook and stir till sauce
boils; simmer 1 to 2 minutes. Pass with duckling. Makes 6 to 8 servings.

PEKING GLAZE

    1 orange
    ½ cup light molasses
    ¼ teaspoon salt
    ¼ teaspoon dry mustard
    ½ teaspoon monosodium glutamate
    ½ teaspoon ground ginger
    ½ teaspoon bottled hot pepper sauce
    1 clove garlic, crushed

Wash orange. With sharp knife, finely sliver
off orange peel to measure 2 tablespoons.
Squeeze orange and measure ½ cup juice. In
saucepan, combine all ingredients. Bring to
boiling; remove from heat.

Use as glaze for broiler-fryer chickens.
Baste chicken occasionally with glaze last 30
minutes of cooking time. Makes 1 cup glaze.

THREE FRUIT STUFFING

    2 cups toasted bread cubes
    ½ cup chopped orange sections
    ½ cup chopped pared apple
    ¼ cup light raisins
    ¼ cup chopped pecans
    ½ teaspoon salt
    ¼ teaspoon ground nutmeg

Toss all ingredients together. Cover and let
stand 1 hour before using. Stir well, then lightly stuff bird. Makes 3 cups stuffing or enough
for a 4- to 5-pound duckling.

TANGY ORANGE STUFFING

Orange marmalade provides the extra zip—

    1 7- or 8-ounce package herb-
       seasoned stuffing
    ½ cup chopped celery
    ¼ cup chopped onion
    ⅓ cup butter or margarine
    ½ cup orange marmalade
    ¼ cup chopped pecans
    1 tablespoon lemon juice
       Dash pepper

Prepare stuffing according to package directions, *omitting* butter. Cook celery and onion
in the ⅓ cup butter or margarine till tender;
add to stuffing along with remaining ingredients; toss lightly. Makes 5 cups of stuffing
or enough for 5-pound duckling.

CRANBERRY STUFFING

    3 cups fresh cranberries
    ¾ cup sugar
    3 quarts slightly dry bread cubes
    1½ to 2 cups raisins
    2 tablespoons grated orange peel
    1 tablespoon salt
    ¾ teaspoon ground cinnamon
    ¾ cup butter, melted
    ¾ cup chicken broth or water

Chop cranberries and stir in sugar. Then combine with bread, raisins, orange peel, salt,
cinnamon, and melted butter. Add broth and
toss lightly to mix. Makes enough stuffing for
10- to 12-pound turkey.

Barbecue roundup

BARBECUED SHORT RIBS

    3 pounds beef short ribs
    1 teaspoon salt
    1 cup chili sauce
    1 12-ounce jar (1 cup) pineapple
      preserves
    ⅓ cup vinegar

Trim excess fat from ribs. Sprinkle meat with salt and dash pepper. Place ribs in Dutch oven. Add ½ cup water; cover and simmer till tender, about 2 hours (add more water during cooking, if needed). Drain. Combine remaining ingredients; coat ribs. Grill over slow coals 15 to 20 minutes, brushing with sauce and turning frequently. Heat remaining glaze and serve with ribs. Serves 3 or 4.

PLUM GLAZED CHICKEN

    1 1-pound 1-ounce jar purple plums
    ¼ teaspoon grated orange peel
    ¼ cup orange juice
    ½ teaspoon ground cinnamon
    ½ teaspoon Worcestershire sauce
    2 2½- to 3-pound ready-to-cook
      broiler-fryer chickens, cut up

Drain plums, reserving ¾ cup syrup. Force plums through sieve; add plum syrup, orange peel and juice, cinnamon, and Worcestershire sauce; mix well. Brush chicken with glaze during last 15 minutes of grilling on each side. Makes 1⅔ cups glaze. Serves 6.

HAM WHEEL ROAST

On a spit, alternate 1-inch slices of fully cooked, boned, rolled ham and fresh pineapple (pared but not cored)—use long holding forks. Stud pineapple with whole cloves. Place on rotisserie with drip pan under roast.

Rotate over hot coals 1½ hours, basting last 30 minutes with Currant Glaze: In small saucepan, break up one 10-ounce jar (1 cup) currant jelly with fork. Add ¼ cup sherry, 1 teaspoon dry mustard, and ¼ teaspoon ground ginger. Cook and stir till smooth.

APPLE-BUTTERED PORK LOIN

    1 5- to 6-pound pork loin, boned,
      rolled, and tied
    ½ cup apple butter
    2 tablespoons peanut butter
    ¼ teaspoon grated orange peel
    2 tablespoons orange juice

Balance roast on spit. Roast over medium coals about 3 hours or till meat thermometer reads 170°. Gradually stir apple butter into peanut butter; add orange peel and juice. Brush over entire surface of roast; continue cooking 15 to 20 minutes. Serves 12 to 16.

BARBECUED SHRIMP

    3 large cloves garlic, sliced
    ¼ cup butter or margarine
    12 ounces cleaned raw shrimp (1½
      pounds in shell)
    ½ lemon, sliced *paper-thin*
      Chopped parsley

Cook garlic in butter 2 or 3 minutes. Line a shallow pan with foil (or use a shallow foil-ware pan); arrange shrimp in a layer over bottom. Dash with salt and pepper. Place lemon slices over shrimp; drizzle with garlic butter; sprinkle with parsley. Cook over hot coals 6 minutes or till done—turn often.

CRANBERRY BURGER SAUCE

    1 1-pound can whole cranberry
      sauce
    ¼ cup finely chopped celery
    1 tablespoon brown sugar
    3 tablespoons Worcestershire sauce
    1 tablespoon salad oil

Combine all ingredients. Grill hamburgers a few minutes on each side before basting with sauce. Makes 2 cups sauce.

Apple-buttered Pork Loin sports a crisp →
Southern-style jacket of peanut and apple butters with a tangy orange accent.

LUAU RIBS

1 13½-ounce can (1⅔ cups)
    crushed pineapple
¼ cup molasses
¼ cup Dijon-style mustard
3 tablespoons lemon juice
3 tablespoons soy sauce
2 tablespoons Worcestershire sauce
1 teaspoon monosodium glutamate
  Dash pepper
4 pounds spareribs *or* loin back ribs

For glaze: Combine first 8 ingredients; set aside. Salt ribs; place bone side down on grill over slow coals. (Watch heat—ribs tend to dry out and char with too much heat.) Grill about 20 minutes; turn meaty side down; grill till browned, about 10 minutes.

Turn meaty side up; brush with glaze; continue grilling without turning for 30 to 45 minutes, till well done. (Loin back ribs take longer.) Slide foil under thinner end of ribs if done before thicker end; continue cooking. Makes 4 to 6 servings.

MINTED LEG OF LAMB

1 6-pound leg of lamb, boned and
    flattened
1 teaspoon monosodium glutamate
½ cup orange marmalade
⅓ cup snipped fresh mint leaves
2 tablespoons snipped chives
½ cup dry red wine

Sprinkle inner surface of meat with monosodium glutamate; season. Combine marmalade, mint, and chives; spread over meat. Roll up roast, tucking in at ends. To tie roast: Wrap cord around meat at one end; tie knot on top. Make a large loop with cord; *twist* at bottom and slide it over end of meat. Repeat, spacing loops at 1½-inch intervals; pull cord up tightly each time. Knot again at end.

Center roast on spit; fasten securely with holding forks. Attach spit and turn on motor (hot coals at back of firebox, drip pan under roast). Roast about 3 hours or till meat thermometer registers 175° to 180°. For the last hour of cooking, pour wine into drip pan and mix with drippings; baste meat with mixture frequently. Skim excess fat from wine mixture and pass with lamb. Makes 10 to 12 servings.

SKEWERED HAM AND FRUIT

  Spiced crab apples
2 to 2½ pounds fully cooked bone-
    less ham, cut in 1½-inch cubes
  Pineapple slices, quartered
½ cup extra-hot catsup
⅓ cup orange marmalade
2 tablespoons finely chopped onion
2 tablespoons salad oil
1 tablespoon lemon juice
1 to 1½ teaspoons dry mustard

Thread apples, ham, and pineapple alternately on skewers. For sauce, combine remaining ingredients. Broil ham and fruit over low coals, 12 to 15 minutes, brushing often with sauce. Use a rotating skewer, or turn skewers frequently during broiling. Serves 6.

HERBED PEAR SAUCE

¾ cup finely chopped onion
1 clove garlic, minced
¼ cup salad oil *or* olive oil
1 12-ounce can (1½ cups) pear
    nectar
½ cup white wine vinegar
¼ cup honey
2 tablespoons Worcestershire sauce
1 teaspoon salt
1 teaspoon dry mustard
1 teaspoon prepared horseradish
½ teaspoon thyme
¼ teaspoon rosemary
¼ teaspoon pepper

Cook onion and garlic in hot oil till tender. Add remaining ingredients; simmer uncovered 5 minutes. Use for marinating and basting chicken or other poultry for barbecue. Heat and pass extra sauce. Makes 3¼ cups.

BARBECUE-APPLE SAUCE

Combine one 8-ounce can (1 cup) applesauce, ¾ cup chili sauce, ¼ cup red wine vinegar, 1 tablespoon brown sugar, 2 teaspoons Worcestershire sauce, ½ teaspoon salt, ¼ teaspoon basil, ⅛ teaspoon pepper, and dash garlic powder. Grill hamburgers or chicken a few minutes on each side before basting with the sauce. Makes 2 cups.

PINEAPPLED SPARERIBS

1 cup pineapple preserves
2 tablespoons vinegar
2 teaspoons Dijon-style mustard
1 teaspoon kitchen bouquet
3 to 4 pounds spareribs

For Pineapple Glaze: Combine first 4 ingredients; set aside. Salt ribs and place bone side down on grill over *slow* coals. (Watch fire—ribs tend to dry out and char.) Broil about 20 minutes; then turn meat side down; broil till nicely browned, about 10 minutes.

Again turn meat side up; continue broiling without turning 30 minutes or till meat is well done (no pink where snipped between the bones). Brush often with Pineapple Glaze. If desired, add hickory (in foil—see below) to coals for smoke flavor. Serves 3 or 4.

Foil Protector: The thinner end of spareribs is likely to get done before the thicker end. When this happens, slide a piece of foil under the thinner end and continue cooking.

Hickory in foil: Good technique for open-grill smoking—air is shut out, so hickory can't blaze. Wrap a fistful of dry hickory chips in foil. Puncture top of package with fork and place on the hot coals. Soon smoke will puff out, continuing for half an hour.

RIBS DEE-LISH

½ cup apricot nectar
½ cup crushed pineapple
½ cup catsup
2 teaspoons lemon juice
½ teaspoon salt
Dash pepper

• • •

3 to 4 pounds meaty spareribs, sawed in lengthwise strips 4 to 5 inches wide

For sauce: Combine first 6 ingredients. Lace ribs on spit, accordion style, and secure with holding forks. Arrange hot coals at back of firebox; place a foil drip pan in front of coals and under ribs. Attach spit, turn on motor, and lower barbecue hood. Let ribs rotate over medium-low coals for 1 to 1¼ hours, or till meat is well done—no pink meat. During the last 15 minutes, brush ribs frequently with sauce. Makes 3 or 4 servings.

ORANGE PORK CURRY

1 4- to 5-pound pork loin roast*
1 orange, cut in thin wedges
1 cup syrup from canned fruit
½ cup brown sugar
¼ cup vinegar
1 tablespoon curry powder
2 tablespoons salad oil
2 tablespoons soy sauce

*Have meatman loosen backbone from ribs, but leave attached. Cut to within 1 inch of backbone in 1-inch chops. In each slit, insert orange wedge, peel side out. Insert skew-

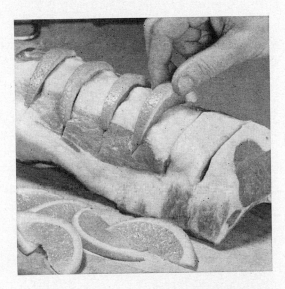

er lengthwise through chops and fruit. Tie roast with cord, end to end, and in 2 or 3 places between. Insert spit; balance roast, securing with holding forks. Season meat.

Roast on rotisserie, with hood down, over *medium* coals for 2 to 2½ hours, or till done. Meanwhile, combine remaining ingredients for sauce. Raise hood during last 30 minutes and brush meat with sauce. Makes 8 servings.

CRANBERRY GRILLED HAM

Beat together one 1-pound can jellied cranberry sauce, ⅓ cup bottled steak sauce, 1 tablespoon brown sugar, 1 tablespoon salad oil, and 2 teaspoons prepared mustard. Slash fat edge of one 1-inch fully cooked ham slice. Broil over *slow* coals 15 to 20 minutes per side. Brush with glaze last 15 minutes.

Sea-going fare

SWEET-SOUR TUNA

Drain one 8¾-ounce can (1 cup) pineapple tidbits, reserving syrup. In saucepan, combine ⅓ *cup* of the pineapple syrup, 1 cup green pepper strips, pineapple tidbits, 1 vegetable bouillon cube, and ½ cup water. Heat mixture to boiling; simmer 5 minutes.

Mix 1 tablespoon cornstarch with remaining pineapple syrup, 1 teaspoon soy sauce, 1 tablespoon vinegar, and 3 tablespoons sugar; stir into pineapple mixture. Cook, stirring constantly, till thickened and bubbling.

Stir in one 6½- or 7-ounce can tuna, drained, and 1 tablespoon butter or margarine. Heat through. Serve on warm chow mein noodles (one 3-ounce can). Serves 4.

TUNA-LEMON LOAF

Place 3 or 4 thin lemon slices in a row in bottom of a *very well-greased* 8½x4½x2½-inch loaf dish. Thoroughly combine two 6½- or 7-ounce cans tuna, drained and finely flaked with one 10½-ounce can condensed cream of celery soup, 3 slightly beaten egg yolks, 1 cup fine cracker crumbs, ¼ cup finely chopped onion, 2 tablespoons chopped canned pimiento, 2 tablespoons snipped parsley, 1 tablespoon lemon juice, and dash pepper.

Fold in 3 stiffly beaten egg whites. Spoon tuna mixture over lemon slices in loaf dish. Bake at 350° for 45 minutes or till center is firm. Invert on warm serving platter. Garnish with parsley and lemon slices. Serves 6.

Mellow blending of flavors in Sweet-sour Tuna makes ordinary ingredients into an excitingly different dish. It's quick and easy to fix, too!

Meat accompaniments

CRANBERRY-DATE RELISH

    1 pound (4 cups) fresh cranberries
    1 cup sugar
    1 cup snipped dates
    ½ cup light raisins
    2 cups water
    ¼ cup vinegar
    ¼ teaspoon ground cinnamon
    ¼ teaspoon ground ginger

In a medium saucepan, combine cranberries, sugar, dates, raisins, water, vinegar, and spices. Bring to boiling and boil rapidly, uncovered, for about 10 minutes, stirring occasionally. Serve chilled. Makes 4 cups.

SPICED GRAPES

    Tokay, Emperor, or Thompson
       seedless green grapes
    5 whole cloves
    5 whole allspice
    2 inches stick cinnamon
    1½ cups sugar
    1 cup white vinegar

Select firm, not overripe, grapes. Leave the grapes on stems; snip into small clusters; wash and drain. Tightly pack grapes and spices into a clean pint jar, being careful not to bruise the fruit. (Or place grapes in a small deep bowl.) Combine sugar and vinegar; heat, stirring till sugar dissolves. Boil 5 minutes. Pour hot syrup over grapes; cover tightly. Refrigerate one or two days. Drain before serving. Makes 1 pint.

PAN-FRIED PAPAYA RINGS

    1 large firm papaya
    2 tablespoons butter or margarine
    Lemon juice

Peel papaya; cut in eight ½-inch crosswise slices; remove seeds. Heat butter till bubbly; add fruit and cook quickly, about 1 minute on each side. Sprinkle with lemon juice. Serve hot with ham or bacon. Makes 4 servings.

ORANGE-SPICED PEACHES

    1 1-pound 13-ounce can peach
       halves
    ½ teaspoon whole cloves
    6 inches stick cinnamon
    10 whole allspice
           • • •
    ⅓ cup vinegar
    ½ cup sugar
    ½ unpeeled orange, quartered and
       sliced

Drain peaches, reserving ½ cup syrup. Tie spices in piece of cheesecloth. In saucepan, combine reserved peach syrup, vinegar, sugar, orange slices, peaches, and spices. Heat to boiling; simmer covered 5 minutes. Let cool to room temperature. Remove spice bag. Serve warm or chilled; stud peaches with a few whole cloves, if desired. Serves 6 to 8.

NECTARINE SAUTE

    3 to 4 nectarines
    2 tablespoons butter or margarine
    2 tablespoons brown sugar
    Lemon juice

Slice nectarines. (Do not peel.) Heat butter and brown sugar in small skillet till bubbly. Add nectarines; cook till heated through and glazed. Sprinkle with lemon juice. Serve hot with ham or bacon. Makes 4 servings.

CURRIED APPLE RELISH

    2 tablespoons butter or margarine
    1 teaspoon sugar
    ½ teaspoon curry powder
    1 1-pound 4-ounce can (2½ cups)
       pie-sliced apples, drained

Melt butter in medium skillet. Stir in sugar and curry powder. Add apples; toss to coat with curry mixture. Cook, stirring occasionally, over low heat till apples are heated through, about 5 minutes. Serve as a relish with meat or poultry. Makes 6 to 8 servings.

48

CRANBERRY-PEACH RELISH

  1 1-pound can cling peach halves
  1 cup sugar
  ¼ cup vinegar
  1 teaspoon whole cloves
  3 inches stick cinnamon
  2 cups fresh cranberries

Drain peaches reserving ⅔ cup syrup. Combine syrup, sugar, vinegar, and spices; bring to boil. Add cranberries; boil without stirring till skins pop, 5 minutes. Add peaches, cut in two. Cool; chill. Makes 3 cups.

CURRANT CHUTNEY

  ½ cup chutney, cut in smaller pieces
  ½ cup red currant jelly
  3 tablespoons dried currants
  2 tablespoons cooking sherry

Thoroughly combine all ingredients. Serve with curried main dishes or baked ham.

FRUIT FRILLS

Kumquat Posies. Make 4 petals by cutting kumquat peel in fourths, from blossom end *almost* to stem end. Peel petals ¾ way back, leaving fruit as center. Chill in ice water 1 hour or till open.
Orange Roses. Cut slice off both ends of orange. Starting at stem end, pare peel in spiral strip, about ½ inch wide. Cut spiral in half. To shape rose, roll peel up tightly, bright orange side out; tack with toothpick. (For larger rose, don't cut spiral in half; roll as above.)
Tangerine Chrysanthemum. Beginning at stem end of tangerine, cut peel down in 6 sections, using kitchen shears, about ¾ way to base. Do not cut into fruit. Gently loosen sections of peel; remove fruit, leaving peel intact. Cut the sections of peel in very fine slivers, only ¾ of way to base. Spread slivered peel apart, sunburst fashion. Repeat with 3 to 5 tangerines; nest slivered peels to make a full-blown chrysanthemum. Fill center with tangerine sections or with raisins and mixed nuts.

CRANBERRY SAUCE

  2 cups sugar
  2 cups water
  1 pound (4 cups) fresh cranberries

Combine sugar and water in saucepan; stir to dissolve sugar. Heat to boiling; boil 5 minutes. Add cranberries; cook till skins pop, about 5 minutes longer. Remove from heat. Serve sauce warm or chilled. Makes 4 cups.

  To mold: Cook about 10 minutes longer or till a drop of sauce jells on a cold plate. Pour into a 4-cup mold. Chill till firm.

SPICED PRUNES

Tart and spicy pickle flavor to accent an attractive fruit platter or tray of cold cuts—

  1 pound (3 cups) dried prunes*
  3½ to 4 cups water
  ½ cup vinegar
  3 inches stick cinnamon
  1 teaspoon whole cloves
  ½ teaspoon whole allspice
  ½ cup brown sugar

Place prunes in saucepan; cover with water; add vinegar and spices. Bring to boiling; reduce heat; cover tightly and simmer till fruit is tender and plump, about 25 minutes. Add sugar; simmer 5 to 10 minutes longer. Cool. Cover and chill 1 or 2 days.

  *Some dried prunes are processed to cut cooking time. Easy way to prepare this type: Place prunes in a container that has a tight-fitting cover. Combine water, vinegar, spices, and sugar; bring to boiling, then pour over prunes. Cover; cool. Chill a day or so. (The longer the prunes soak the plumper they get.)

BAKED CHUTNEY PEACHES

  6 canned peach halves
  1 tablespoon melted butter
  6 tablespoons chutney

Place drained peaches, cut side up, on cake rack. Brush with melted butter. Spoon 1 tablespoon chutney into center of each peach half. Bake in baking dish at 350° for 10 to 15 minutes or till heated through. Serve hot.

Hawaiian Beets and Sweet Potatoes Royale highlight tasty fruit and vegetable duos. **Hawaiian Beets:** In saucepan, combine 2 tablespoons brown sugar, 1 tablespoon cornstarch, and ¼ teaspoon salt. Stir in one 8¾ ounce can pineapple tidbits. Cook and stir till mixture thickens and bubbles. Add 1 tablespoon butter, 1 tablespoon lemon juice, and one 1-pound can (2 cups) sliced beets, drained. Cook over medium heat about 5 minutes, or till heated through. Serves 4 or 5.

APRICOT SWEET POTATOES

    1 1-pound 1-ounce can vacuum
       packed sweet potatoes, sliced
 1¼ cups brown sugar
 1½ tablespoons cornstarch
    1 teaspoon grated orange peel
  ¼ teaspoon salt
  ⅛ teaspoon ground cinnamon
    1 1-pound 1-ounce can apricot
       halves
    2 tablespoons butter or margarine
  ½ cup pecan halves

Arrange potatoes in lightly greased 10x6x1½-inch baking dish. Combine next 5 ingredients. Drain apricots, reserving 1 cup syrup; add syrup to sugar mixture. Cook and stir over medium heat; simmer 3 minutes. Add apricots, butter, and pecans; bring to boiling; boil 2 minutes. Pour over potatoes. Bake, uncovered, at 375° for 25 minutes. Serves 6.

SUMMERTIME CARROTS

Cook 2 cups sliced carrots in ¼ cup beef broth till tender-crisp, 8 to 10 minutes. Blend 1 teaspoon cornstarch with 2 tablespoons sauterne; stir into carrots; add 1 cup seedless green grapes, 1 tablespoon butter, ½ teaspoon lemon juice, ¼ teaspoon salt, and dash pepper. Cook and stir till boiling. Serves 4.

SWEET POTATOES ROYALE

    1 1-pound can whole sweet
       potatoes, drained
  ½ cup brown sugar
    1 tablespoon cornstarch
  ¼ teaspoon salt
    1 cup orange juice
  ¼ cup light raisins
    2 tablespoons dry sherry
       California walnut halves
  ½ teaspoon shredded orange peel

Arrange sweet potatoes in shallow baking dish. Dash with salt. In saucepan, mix sugar, cornstarch, and salt; blend in juice; add raisins. Cook and stir over high heat to boiling. Add remaining ingredients; pour over potatoes. Bake, uncovered, at 350° for 25 to 30 minutes, or till well glazed. Makes 4 servings.

SALADS
AND
DRESSINGS

*Tangerine Walnut Toss,
featuring sunny,
Dancy tangerines in a crisp
green salad, is one of
the many fruit-laden salads
in this chapter.
Fruit dressings, too!*

Luscious fruit salads

TANGERINE WALNUT TOSS

   7 cups torn lettuce (about 1 head)
   2 cups tangerine sections
   ½ mild white onion, sliced and
      separated in rings
   ⅓ cup Italian dressing
      Walnut croutons

Toss lettuce, tangerine sections, and onion rings with Italian dressing. Top with *Walnut Croutons:* Melt 1 tablespoon butter over medium heat. Add ¼ teaspoon salt and ½ cup California walnut pieces. Stir till walnuts are crisp and butter-browned. Serves 6 to 8.

GREEN AND GOLD SALAD

   1   cup salad oil
   ⅓   cup tarragon vinegar
   ¼   cup sugar
   1   tablespoon lime juice
   ½   teaspoon *each* salt, dry mustard,
       and instant minced onion
   1½ tablespoons fresh papaya seeds
   1   papaya, peeled and sliced
       lengthwise
   ½   medium cucumber, sliced
   3   cups mixed salad greens

Place salad oil, vinegar, sugar, lime juice, salt, mustard, and onion in blender; blend thoroughly. Add papaya seeds and blend till seeds are size of coarsely ground pepper; chill. Makes 1½ cups. Combine papaya, cucumber, and greens. Toss lightly with desired amount of dressing. Makes 4 servings.

MELON WEDGES

Slice honeydew melons into quarters; seed. Fill hollow with fresh blueberries and sliced bananas. Spoon Honey Dressing atop fruit.
Honey Dressing: Combine ½ cup dairy sour cream, ¼ teaspoon dry mustard, and 1½ to 2 tablespoons honey. Beat well. Add ½ teaspoon grated orange peel and dash salt; slowly beat in 1 tablespoon orange juice and 1 teaspoon lemon juice; chill. Makes ¾ cup.

BERRY-PATCH SALAD

   2 cantaloupes, chilled and halved
   1 12-ounce carton (1½ cups)
      cream-style cottage cheese
   1 8¾-ounce can (1 cup) pineapple
      tidbits, chilled and drained
   ½ cup halved strawberries
   ½ cup red raspberries

Remove seeds and loosen cantaloupes from rind by cutting around with grapefruit knife. With paring knife, cut fruit in wedges, spoke fashion, by cutting to, but not through, sides and bottom of melon.

Combine cottage cheese and pineapple; spoon into melon halves. Top with strawberries and raspberries. Makes 4 servings.

LUNCHEON COOLER

   2 ripe peaches, peeled
   2 bananas, peeled and sliced
   ½ cup blueberries
   3 tablespoons honey
   2 to 3 teaspoons finely chopped
      candied ginger
   2 cantaloupes, chilled and halved
      Lime sherbet

Slice 1 peach; set aside for garnish. Dice remaining peach into large bowl. (Sprinkle peaches and brush banana slices with color keeper or lemon juice to prevent browning.) Add banana slices, blueberries, honey, and ginger; toss lightly to mix and to coat fruit. Remove cantaloupe seeds; spoon fruit mixture into center.

Rim with peach slices; top with generous scoop of lime sherbet and garnish with additional blueberries. Makes 4 servings.

NUT-CRUSTED BANANAS

Peel fully ripe bananas. Cut in half lengthwise and crosswise. Dip in a mixture of equal parts honey and lime juice. Arrange on plate and sprinkle generously with chopped macadamia nuts or California walnuts.

Bring the lush gay atmosphere of the islands to your table with this bright Hawaiian Fruit Plate accented with fresh limes and dressing.

PEACH-PRUNE SALAD

- 1 8-ounce package cream cheese
- ¼ cup light cream
- ½ teaspoon curry powder
- ¼ cup chopped raisins
- 2 tablespoons chopped salted peanuts
- 1 tablespoon finely chopped candied ginger
  Chilled canned or cooked prunes, well drained and pitted
  Chilled canned peach halves, well drained

Soften cream cheese and blend with cream and curry; add raisins, nuts, and candied ginger. Fill prunes generously; center a stuffed prune in each peach half. For each serving, arrange 2 peach-prune stack-ups on a lettuce ruffle. Makes about 1⅓ cups filling.

HAWAIIAN FRUIT PLATE

Have salad ingredients chilled. Pare 1 small pineapple; cut in 6 spears and remove core. Cut rind from 6 watermelon wedges. Halve 1 medium papaya and scoop out seeds; cut in 6 wedges and remove rind. Brush 3 fully ripe bananas, peeled and quartered, with pineapple or lime juice. Drain one 1-pound can (2 cups) sliced peaches. Line large chilled platter with romaine. Arrange fruits atop, spoke fashion. Garnish with 2 limes, cut in slices and wedges, and ½ pint fresh whole strawberries. Pass a cruet of Pineapple-french Dressing. Makes 6 servings.

Pineapple-french Dressing: Combine 1 cup salad oil, ¼ cup pineapple juice, ¼ cup lime juice, 1 tablespoon vinegar, ⅓ cup sugar, 1½ teaspoons paprika, and 1 teaspoon salt; cover and shake. Chill. Shake again just before serving. Makes 1¾ cups dressing.

CRANBERRY WALDORF

    2 cups fresh cranberries
    3 cups miniature marshmallows
    ¾ cup sugar
    2 cups diced unpared tart apple
    ½ cup seedless green grapes
    ½ cup broken California walnuts
    ¼ teaspoon salt
    1 cup whipping cream, whipped

Grind cranberries and combine with marshmallows and sugar. Cover and chill overnight. Add apple, grapes, walnuts, and salt. Fold in whipped cream; chill. Serve in large bowl or individual lettuce cups. Garnish with clusters of grapes. Makes 8 to 10 servings.

HAWAIIAN WALDORF SALAD

    1 8¾-ounce can crushed pineapple
    ½ cup light raisins
    2 cups fresh or frozen pineapple
       chunks, *well* drained
    2 cups diced celery
    1 cup mayonnaise

Drain *crushed* pineapple *well*, reserving syrup. Add raisins to syrup and heat just to boiling; remove from heat and let stand 10 minutes to plump raisins; drain. Mix pineapple chunks, celery, and drained raisins. Combine crushed pineapple and mayonnaise; add to salad and toss lightly. Chill. Arrange in lettuce-lined bowl. Makes 6 servings.

PEAR BLUE CHEESE SALAD

    3 cups diced unpared pears
    1 cup diced celery
    ½ cup broken California walnuts
    1 ounce blue cheese, crumbled
       (¼ cup)
    ¼ cup dairy sour cream
    ¼ cup mayonnaise or salad dressing

Combine pears, celery, and nuts. Blend remaining ingredients and dash salt; toss lightly with pear mixture. Serves 6 to 8.

← Choose a good "eating apple," juicy and with plenty of crunch, to make this Waldorf Salad. Frosted grapes add sparkle.

Above: Whether you pare the apples for Waldorf Salad is up to you, but it's easier to core and slice them before dicing.

Below: For julienne-cut celery, cut stalk in 3 or 4 long strips, then cut on bias several strips at once in 1-inch pieces.

WALDORF SALAD

    2 cups diced apple
    1 cup julienne-cut celery
    ½ cup broken California walnuts
    ¼ cup mayonnaise
    1 tablespoon sugar
    ½ teaspoon lemon juice
    ½ cup whipping cream, whipped

Combine first 3 ingredients. Blend together next 3 ingredients and dash salt. Fold in whipped cream; fold into apple mixture; chill. Arrange in lettuce-lined bowl. Decorate with frosted grapes. Serves 6.

CRANBERRY-APRICOT SALAD

    1 1-pound jar refrigerated fruit
        salad
    1 1-pound can jellied cranberry
        sauce, chilled
    1 cup seedless green grapes
    1 1-pound 6-ounce can apricot pie
        filling
    1 cup miniature marshmallows
    ½ cup chopped pecans

Drain fruit salad thoroughly. Cut cranberry
sauce into ½-inch cubes and add to fruit
salad. Fold in grapes, apricot pie filling, and
marshmallows. Chill thoroughly, about 4 to 5
hours. Just before serving, stir in the chopped
pecans. Makes 6 to 8 servings.

CRANBERRY COLESLAW

Combine ¼ cup sliced fresh cranberries, 1
tablespoon honey, and 1 teaspoon celery seed;
let stand 15 minutes. Add ¼ cup mayonnaise
and 1 teaspoon vinegar; mix well. Pour over
3 cups crisp finely shredded cabbage; toss
lightly. Salt to taste. Serves 4 or 5.

PINEAPPLE OUTRIGGER

    1 large orange
    2 small ripe pineapples
    ½ cup halved seedless green grapes
    ½ cup sliced celery
    3 cups diced cooked chicken
    1 cup whipping cream, whipped
    ½ cup mayonnaise or salad dressing
    ¾ teaspoon salt
    ¼ teaspoon marjoram
    ¼ teaspoon rosemary
    ½ cup slivered almonds, toasted

Have salad ingredients chilled. Section
orange, reserving 2 tablespoons juice for
dressing. Dice orange sections. Cut pine-
apples (including crowns) in half. Hollow
out, leaving shell ½ inch thick. Remove core.
Dice pineapple and combine with orange,
grapes, celery, and chicken. Fold whipped
cream into mayonnaise; add reserved orange
juice and seasonings. Fold into chicken mixture; pile into pineapple shells. Trim with almonds and green grapes. Serves 4.

24-HOUR SALAD

    1 1-pound 4½-ounce can pineapple
        tidbits
    1 1-pound can light sweet cherries,
        pitted
    3 egg yolks
    2 tablespoons vinegar
    2 tablespoons sugar
        Dash salt
    1 tablespoon butter or margarine
    2 medium oranges, pared and diced
    2 cups miniature marshmallows *or*
        16 regular, cut in eighths
    1 cup whipping cream, whipped

Drain pineapple, reserving 2 tablespoons
syrup. Drain cherries. In top of double boiler,
beat egg yolks slightly; add reserved pineapple syrup, vinegar, sugar, salt, and butter.
Place over *hot, not boiling water;* cook, stirring
constantly, till mixture *thickens slightly* and
barely coats a spoon (about 12 minutes). Cool
to room temperature.

Combine well-drained oranges, pineapple,
cherries, and the marshmallows. Pour custard
over and mix gently. Fold in whipped cream.
Pour into serving bowl.* Cover and chill 24
hours. Trim with fresh strawberry halves and
seedless green grapes. Makes 6 to 8 servings.

*Or chill in mixing bowl; before serving,
gently lift out into serving bowl.

FESTIVE FRUIT SALAD

    1 1-pound can light sweet cherries,
        pitted
    1 1-pound can dark sweet cherries,
        pitted
    1 1-pound can sliced peaches
    1 1-pound can pears, quartered
    1 13½-ounce can pineapple chunks
    1 cup miniature marshmallows
    ½ cup dairy sour cream
    1 cup whipping cream, whipped

Drain cherries, peaches, pears, and pineapple
thoroughly and combine in a large bowl.
Blend together remaining ingredients; fold
into fruit. Chill overnight. Serves 12 to 15.

Luscious 24-Hour Salad can be made the →
day before and brought to the table as the
salad-dessert to complete a jiffy meal.

58

Serve Crab Luncheon Salad in an unusual bowl
—a Persian melon shell. Vary the fruits in the
Buffet Fruit Medley to keep up with the season.

CRAB LUNCHEON SALAD

  1 7½-ounce can crab meat, well
      drained and flaked
  ½ cup sliced celery
  2 tablespoons sliced ripe olives
  1 tablespoon sliced green onion
  ¼ teaspoon salt
  ¼ teaspoon monosodium glutamate
  ½ cup mayonnaise or salad dressing
  3 hard-cooked eggs, sliced
  1 medium Persian melon, chilled

Combine first 6 ingredients and dash pepper; fold in mayonnaise and 2 of the sliced eggs. Chill. Using a sawtooth cut, remove top third of melon; remove seeds. With grapefruit knife, loosen melon meat from rind. Slice meat into sections and serve with salad. Sprinkle inside of melon with lemon juice. Fill with salad. Trim with egg. Serves 4.

BUFFET FRUIT MEDLEY

Using a sawtooth cut, remove top third of a large, well-chilled, oblong watermelon. (Use paper pattern to trace cutting lines so cuts are uniform.) Chill top third of melon to serve another time. Carefully scoop out melon meat and cut into chunks. Combine melon chunks with washed, hulled, and halved strawberries, sliced peaches (if fresh, use color keeper or lemon juice), greengage plums, pitted and sliced, and blueberries. Pile fruits into melon "boat." Serve with Dressing.

Avocado Cream Dressing: Whip 1 cup whipping cream with 2 tablespoons confectioners' sugar and ¼ to ½ teaspoon salt; fold in 2 medium avocados, halved, seeded, peeled, and mashed (about ¾ cup) and 1 tablespoon finely chopped candied ginger. (If dressing is made ahead of time, mash avocado and add just before serving.) Makes 2 cups.

CURRIED CHICKEN ROUNDS

These look like little cakes and make perfect luncheon salads. Make ahead; chill till serving time—

- ¾ cup diced cooked chicken
- ½ cup finely chopped celery
- ¼ cup finely chopped walnuts
- 1 tablespoon instant minced onion
- 1 tablespoon lemon juice
- ½ teaspoon curry powder
- ⅓ cup mayonnaise or salad dressing
- 12 slices sandwich bread
- 1 1-pound 4½-ounce can pineapple slices, well drained (reserve syrup)
- 1 8-ounce package cream cheese

Combine first 7 ingredients; add salt and pepper to taste. Cut bread in rounds same size as pineapple rings. Lightly butter bread. Spread chicken salad on *half* of the bread rounds. Top with remaining bread rounds. Place each sandwich atop a pineapple ring. Soften cheese with 2 to 3 tablespoons pineapple syrup. Spread on tops and sides of sandwiches. Garnish with pineapple sections and walnut halves. Makes 6 salads.

CORONADO SALAD

- 2 medium cantaloupes
- 2 cups diced cooked chicken
- ½ cup chopped celery
- ½ cup halved seedless green grapes
- 2 tablespoons sliced pimiento-stuffed green olives
- ½ teaspoon monosodium glutamate
- ½ teaspoon salt
  Dash white pepper
- ½ cup whipping cream
- ¼ cup mayonnaise or salad dressing

Halve cantaloupes crosswise; remove seeds. Loosen fruit by cutting around with grapefruit knife. With paring knife, cut fruit in wedges, spoke fashion, cutting to, but not through, the rind. Chill. Toss next 7 ingredients lightly to mix. At serving time, whip cream and mix with mayonnaise; fold into chicken mixture. Spoon into melon halves. Garnish with hard-cooked egg slices, toasted sliced almonds, additional sliced stuffed green olives, and grapes. Makes 4 servings.

CHUTNEY CHICKEN SALAD

Mix together ¾ cup mayonnaise or salad dressing, ½ cup chutney, ¼ cup dark raisins, ½ cup salted peanuts, and ½ cup flaked coconut. Toss with 2 cups coarsely diced cooked chicken and ½ teaspoon salt. Line 4 salad plates with lettuce. Spoon salad into each. Slice 2 bananas diagonally; cut 1 avocado into lengthwise slices. Dip fruits in lemon juice; arrange around salads. Serves 4.

CRAB-STUFFED AVOCADOS

- ½ cup mayonnaise or salad dressing
- 2 hard-cooked eggs, chopped
- ¼ cup chopped celery
- 3 tablespoons chopped pimiento
- 1 teaspoon dry mustard
- ¼ teaspoon salt
  Dash Worcestershire sauce
- 3 medium avocados
- ¾ pound chilled, cooked, shelled crab legs (about 1½ pounds in shell), cut in short lengths

Combine mayonnaise, eggs, celery, pimiento, mustard, salt, and Worcestershire sauce. Chill.

Halve avocado lengthwise; carefully twist to remove seed. Brush avocados with lemon or lime juice to retain color. Fill avocados with egg mixture and top with crab. Serve with lemon wedges. Makes 6 servings.

APPLE TUNA TOSS

- 1 medium head lettuce, torn in bite-size pieces (4 cups)
- 2 cups diced apple
- 1 11-ounce can (1⅓ cups) mandarin orange sections, drained
- 1 6½- or 7-ounce can tuna, drained and broken in large chunks
- ⅓ cup coarsely chopped walnuts
- ½ cup mayonnaise or salad dressing
- 2 teaspoons soy sauce
- 1 teaspoon lemon juice

In a large salad bowl, combine lettuce, apple, orange sections, tuna, and nuts; toss together. Combine mayonnaise, soy sauce, and lemon juice; mix well. To serve, add dressing to salad; toss gently. Makes 4 to 6 servings.

Shimmery molded salads

CHICKEN MELON MOUSSE

- 1 large cantaloupe
- 1 medium cucumber
- ½ cup mayonnaise or salad dressing
- ⅓ cup lemon juice
- 2 tablespoons vinegar
- 1 teaspoon salt
- 2 cups finely chopped cooked chicken
- 2 envelopes (2 tablespoons) unflavored gelatin
- ½ cup cold water
- ½ cup whipping cream, whipped

Halve cantaloupe; remove the seeds and rind. Coarsely shred melon meat to make 2 cups drained melon; reserve juice. Add water to melon juice, if necessary, to make 1 cup. Halve cucumber lengthwise and remove seeds, but do not pare; shred to make 1 cup.

Combine mayonnaise, lemon juice, vinegar, and salt; stir in melon, cucumber, and chicken. Soften gelatin in the cold water. Add to melon juice; cook and stir over low heat till gelatin dissolves. Stir into melon mixture, mixing well. Chill till partially set.

Fold in whipped cream. Turn into 6- or 6½-cup ring mold; chill till firm, 8 hours or overnight. Unmold on chilled plate.

If desired, fill center of ring with cucumber slices and cantaloupe cubes; trim plate with endive. Pass toasted slivered almonds to spoon over each serving. Serves 6 to 8.

CRANBERRY MARBLE MOLD

- 2 3-ounce packages cherry-flavored gelatin
- 2 cups boiling water
- 1 8¾-ounce can crushed pineapple
- 1 1-pound can whole cranberry sauce
- 1 cup dairy sour cream

Dissolve gelatin in boiling water. Stir in pineapple. Chill until partially set. Fold in cranberry sauce. Spoon into 8x8x2-inch pan. Spoon sour cream atop; stir through to marble. Chill till firm. Serves 6 to 8.

RED-JEWELED HONEYDEW

- 1 large or 2 small honeydew melons
- 1 3-ounce package raspberry-flavored gelatin
- ¾ cup boiling water
- 1 10-ounce package frozen raspberries, partially thawed
- ¼ cup port
- 1 tablespoon lime juice
  Dash salt

Cut a 2½-inch plug in one end of melon. With long-handled spoon, remove seeds. Turn melon upside down on paper toweling to drain. Dissolve gelatin in the boiling water; add raspberries, wine, lime juice, and salt. Chill till mixture is partially set.

Cut bottom from small paper cup to make a funnel. Prop melon upright in small bowl. Pour gelatin through paper-cup funnel into melon. (Mold any extra gelatin in individual salad molds.) Replace plug in top of melon and chill till firm, overnight. Carefully slice melon into wedges; serve with lime wedges and green grapes. Makes 4 to 6 servings.

APPLESAUCE-PEACH SALAD

- 1 3-ounce package lemon-flavored gelatin
- 1½ cups boiling water
- 1 cup applesauce
- ½ cup chopped pecans
- 1 large fresh peach, peeled and sliced or 1 12-ounce package frozen sliced peaches*

Dissolve gelatin in the boiling water. Chill till partially set. Stir in remaining ingredients. Turn into 8x8x2-inch dish; chill till set, 3 to 4 hours. Makes 6 servings.

*If using frozen peaches, thaw and drain, reserving ½ cup syrup. *Dissolve gelatin in 1 cup boiling water instead of 1½ cups;* add reserved peach syrup. Continue as above.

Great summer fare! Red-jeweled Honeydew sparkles with raspberries; Chicken Melon Mousse features cantaloupe.

CRAN-RASPBERRY RING

You'll enjoy the refreshing tartness of this easy make-ahead salad—

1 3-ounce package raspberry-
    flavored gelatin
1 3-ounce package lemon-flavored
    gelatin
2 cups boiling water
1 10-ounce package frozen
    raspberries
1 14-ounce jar (1⅛ cups)
    cranberry-orange relish
1 7-ounce bottle (about 1 cup)
    lemon-lime carbonated beverage

Dissolve raspberry- and lemon-flavored gelatins in boiling water. Stir in frozen raspberries, breaking up large pieces with fork. Add cranberry-orange relish. Chill till cold but not set. Resting bottle on rim of bowl, carefully pour in lemon-lime carbonated beverage; stir gently with up and down motion. Chill till partially set. Turn into a 6- or 6½-cup ring mold. Chill till firm, about 4 hours. Unmold on crisp greens. Makes 8 to 10 servings.

MOLDED RUBY RED SALAD

A crown of avocado slices sets off this salad—

2 cups cranberry-juice cocktail
2 3-ounce packages raspberry-
    flavored gelatin
1 8¾-ounce can (1 cup)
    pineapple tidbits
½ cup port
½ cup water
1 avocado, peeled and sliced
1 cup diced pared apple
½ cup finely chopped celery
    Fresh grapefruit sections

Heat cranberry juice to boiling. Add gelatin, stirring till dissolved. Add pineapple tidbits (undrained), wine, and water. Arrange avocado slices in bottom of 5-cup mold. Pour enough gelatin mixture over slices to cover; chill till almost set. Chill remaining cranberry mixture till partially set; fold in apple and celery. Pour over avocado layer. Chill till firm. Unmold and garnish with grapefruit sections. Makes 8 to 10 servings.

PINEAPPLE-BEET MOLD

1 1-pound can shoestring beets
1 8¾-ounce can crushed pineapple
2 3-ounce packages lemon-flavored
    gelatin
2 cups boiling water
2 tablespoons lemon juice
    Dash salt

Drain beets and pineapple, reserving 1½ cups combined liquid. Dissolve gelatin in boiling water. Add reserved liquid, lemon juice, and salt. Mix well. Chill till partially set. Fold in drained beets and pineapple. Pour into 6-cup ring mold. Chill till set. Serve with horse-radish-spiked mayonnaise. Serves 8 to 10.

CRANBERRY-AVOCADO MOLD

2 3-ounce packages raspberry-
    flavored gelatin
2 cups boiling water
1½ cups cold water
1 cup fresh cranberries, ground
½ cup sugar
    Dash salt
1 avocado, peeled and cubed
¼ cup chopped California walnuts

Dissolve gelatin in boiling water; add cold water. Chill till partially set. Combine cranberries, sugar, salt, avocado, and nuts; fold into gelatin. Pour into 6½-cup mold; chill till firm. Makes 8 servings.

APPLE-RHUBARB MOLD

1 12-ounce package frozen rhubarb
2 3-ounce packages raspberry-
    flavored gelatin
1 12-ounce can (1½ cups)
    unsweetened pineapple juice
½ cup water
2 cups chopped apple

Cook rhubarb according to package directions. Stir in gelatin; cook and stir over medium heat till gelatin dissolves. Stir in pineapple juice and the water. Chill till mixture is partially set. Stir in chopped apple. Spoon into a 5½-cup ring mold. Chill till firm, 4 to 6 hours. Makes 8 to 10 servings.

Children like Strawberry-banana Mold—
two favorite fruits plus whipped cream!

PEAR-PINEAPPLE RING

1 1-pound 13-ounce can (3½ cups)
   pear halves
1 3-ounce package orange-
   pineapple-flavored gelatin
1 cup boiling water
2 tablespoons lemon juice
¼ teaspoon salt
¼ teaspoon ground ginger
¼ cup chopped California walnuts
1 3-ounce package cream cheese,
   softened
5 canned pineapple slices, halved
   Thin strips pimiento

Drain pears, reserving 1 cup syrup. Dissolve
gelatin in boiling water. Stir in reserved
pear syrup, lemon juice, salt, and ginger.
Chill till partially set. Meanwhile, stir nuts
into cream cheese; shape in small balls; place
one in center of each pear half.

Overlap pineapple slices and pear halves
in 6½-cup ring mold with cut side of pear
toward center. Arrange pimiento strips between. Pour gelatin mixture over all. Chill
until firm. Makes 8 to 10 servings.

APPLE-AVOCADO RING

1 3-ounce package strawberry-
   flavored gelatin
1 cup boiling water
1 15-ounce jar spiced apple rings
1 3-ounce package lemon-flavored
   gelatin
1 cup boiling water
½ cup cold water
1 tablespoon lemon juice
2 avocados, peeled and mashed
   (1 cup)
½ cup whipping cream, whipped

Dissolve strawberry gelatin in boiling water.
Drain apple rings, reserving ¼ cup syrup.
Add water to make 1 cup; add to gelatin.
Chill till partially set. Dice apple rings, re-
serving 3 for garnish. Fold in apples. Pour in-
to 6½-cup ring mold. Chill till almost set.

Dissolve lemon gelatin in boiling water.
Add cold water and lemon juice. Chill till
partially set. Fold in avocado and whipped
cream. Pour over first layer. Chill till set.
Trim with apple rings. Serves 8 to 10.

STRAWBERRY-BANANA MOLD

Dissolve two 3-ounce packages strawberry-
flavored gelatin in 2 cups boiling water; stir
to dissolve gelatin. Thaw one 10-ounce package frozen strawberries *just enough* to drain off
1 tablespoon syrup; reserve the 1 tablespoon
syrup. Add berries to gelatin; break in small
chunks with fork; stir to completely thaw
berries. Add 1 cup cold water. Chill till
partially set.

Slice 2 bananas on the bias into gelatin;
stir gently to distribute fruit. Turn into a 6-
cup fluted mold. Chill till set, about 6 hours.
Unmold; garnish with greens and banana
slices. Top with Strawberry Whipped Cream:
Stir reserved strawberry syrup into 1 cup
whipping cream, whipped. Serves 8 to 10.

CRANBERRY CHEESE MOLD

1 3-ounce package orange-
    pineapple-flavored gelatin
1 cup orange juice
1 2-ounce package dessert topping
    mix
1 3-ounce package cream cheese,
    softened
¼ cup chopped pecans
1 envelope (1 tablespoon)
    unflavored gelatin
¼ cup cold water
1 1-pound can whole cranberry
    sauce
2 tablespoons lemon juice
¼ teaspoon ground allspice
⅛ teaspoon ground nutmeg
1 cup orange sections
1 7-ounce bottle ginger ale

Dissolve orange-pineapple gelatin in 1 cup
boiling water. Stir in orange juice. Chill till
partially set. Prepare dessert topping mix according to package directions. Blend in
cheese; add nuts; fold into gelatin. Pour into
9x9x2-inch dish. Chill till almost firm.

Soften unflavored gelatin in cold water;
dissolve over hot water. Combine remaining
ingredients. Stir in gelatin mixture. Pour over
top of first layer. Chill firm. Serves 8 to 10.

PINEAPPLE-RHUBARB RING

1 1-pound 4½-ounce can (2½ cups)
    pineapple tidbits
2 cups 1-inch slices fresh rhubarb
⅓ cup sugar
½ cup water
2 3-ounce packages cherry-flavored
    gelatin
1 tablespoon lemon juice
½ cup broken pecans

Drain pineapple, reserving syrup. Combine
rhubarb, sugar, and water; cover and cook
just till tender, about 5 minutes. Drain
thoroughly, reserving syrup. Combine pineapple and rhubarb syrups; add water to make
3½ cups. Heat to boiling; add gelatin and
stir to dissolve. Add lemon juice; cool. Chill
till partially set. Fold in pineapple, rhubarb,
and nuts; pour into 6-cup ring mold. Chill
firm. Makes 8 to 10 servings.

RED RASPBERRY RING

1 10-ounce package frozen
    raspberries, thawed
2 3-ounce packages red raspberry-
    flavored gelatin
2 cups boiling water
1 pint vanilla ice cream
1 6-ounce can (¾ cup) frozen pink
    lemonade concentrate, thawed
¼ cup chopped pecans

Drain raspberries, reserving syrup. Dissolve
gelatin in boiling water. Add ice cream by
spoonfuls, stirring till melted. Stir in lemonade concentrate and the reserved syrup. Chill
till partially set. Fold in raspberries and pecans. Turn into 6-cup ring mold. Chill till
firm. Makes 8 to 10 servings.

LEMON APPLE SALAD

1 3-ounce package lemon-flavored
    gelatin
1½ cups boiling water
½ cup dairy sour cream
1 medium apple, quartered, cored,
    and grated (1 cup)

Dissolve gelatin in boiling water. Blend in
sour cream. Chill till partially set. Fold in
grated apple. Pour into 3-cup ring mold. Chill
till set. Makes 4 or 5 servings.

CHERRY MINCEMEAT MOLD

1 1-pound can (2 cups) pitted
    dark sweet cherries
2 3-ounce packages cherry-flavored
    gelatin
2 cups boiling water
2 tablespoons lemon juice
½ cup prepared mincemeat
½ cup diced apple
½ cup chopped nuts

Drain cherries, reserving syrup. Cut cherries
in half. Dissolve gelatin in boiling water. Add
enough water to reserved syrup to make 1¾
cups; stir into gelatin; add lemon juice. Chill
till partially set; fold in cherries, mincemeat,
apple, and nuts. Pour into 6½-cup mold;
chill firm. Serves 8 to 10.

FROSTED BERRY SQUARES

1 13½-ounce can (1⅔ cups) crushed pineapple
2 3-ounce packages lemon-flavored gelatin
1 7-ounce bottle (about 1 cup) ginger ale
1 1-pound can (2 cups) jellied cranberry sauce
1 2-ounce package dessert topping mix
1 8-ounce package cream cheese, softened
½ cup chopped pecans
1 tablespoon butter or margarine

Drain pineapple, reserving syrup. Add water to syrup to make 1 cup; heat to boiling. Dissolve gelatin in hot liquid; cool. Gently stir in ginger ale; chill till partially set.

Meanwhile, blend drained pineapple and cranberry sauce; fold into gelatin mixture. Turn into 9x9x2-inch dish; chill till firm. Prepare dessert topping using package directions; blend in cream cheese; spread over gelatin.

Toast pecans in butter in moderate oven (350°) about 10 minutes; sprinkle over top of salad. Chill. Makes 9 servings.

SPICED MANDARIN MOLD

The flavor bouquet makes this salad extra special—

1 11-ounce can (1⅓ cups) mandarin orange sections
¼ teaspoon salt
6 inches stick cinnamon
½ teaspoon whole cloves
2 3-ounce packages orange-flavored gelatin
2 cups cold water
3 tablespoons lemon juice
½ cup broken California walnuts

Drain oranges, reserving syrup. Add water to syrup to make 1¾ cups. In saucepan, combine syrup mixture, salt, and spices. Cover and simmer 10 minutes; remove from heat; let stand covered 10 minutes to steep. Strain.

Add gelatin to syrup mixture; stir over low heat till gelatin is dissolved. Add cold water and lemon juice. Chill till partially set. Stir in oranges and nuts; turn into a 6 cup mold. Chill till firm. Serves 6 to 8.

CITRUS PERFECTION SALAD

1 3-ounce package lemon-flavored gelatin
1 cup boiling water
1 tablespoon vinegar
¼ teaspoon salt
1 1-pound can grapefruit sections
1 cup finely shredded crisp cabbage
¼ cup finely chopped celery
2 tablespoons sliced pimiento-stuffed green olives

Dissolve gelatin in boiling water; add vinegar and salt. Drain grapefruit, reserving syrup. Add water to syrup to make 1 cup; add to gelatin. Chill till partially set.

Fold in grapefruit, cabbage, celery, and olives. Turn into a 1-quart mold. Chill till firm. Unmold on greens. Makes 6 servings.

BERRY-RHUBARB MOLD

Cook one 1-pound package frozen rhubarb according to package directions. Add two 3-ounce packages strawberry-flavored gelatin; stir till dissolved. Stir in one 13½-ounce can crushed pineapple; chill till partially set. Fold in one 10-ounce package frozen strawberries, thawed. Turn into 6 or 8 individual molds. Chill till set. Serves 6 to 8.

AVOCADO-CITRUS SALAD

1 8½-ounce can grapefruit sections
2 3-ounce packages orange-pineapple-flavored gelatin
2 cups boiling water
1 7-ounce bottle (about 1 cup) ginger ale
2 avocados, halved, peeled, and sliced crosswise

Drain grapefruit, reserving syrup; add water to syrup to make ¾ cup. Dice grapefruit sections. Dissolve gelatin in the boiling water. Add syrup mixture to the dissolved gelatin; cool. Add ginger ale, stirring gently, with an up-and-down motion. Chill till partially set. Fold in diced grapefruit sections and sliced avocado. Pour into 6½-cup ring mold. Chill 6 to 8 hours or overnight. Unmold on salad greens. Makes 8 to 10 servings.

Glistening crown of lime gelatin tops Spring Salad Ring. Pineapple and cucumber add contrasting crunch to the creamy cheese layer.

SPRING SALAD RING

Dissolve two 3-ounce packages lime-flavored gelatin in 1¾ cups boiling water; add ¼ cup lemon juice. For clear gelatin layer: Measure ¾ cup of the gelatin mixture and to it add ¼ cup water; pour into 6-cup ring mold. Chill till almost set.

Meanwhile, prepare pineapple-cucumber gelatin layer: Pare 1 large cucumber; halve and scrape out seeds. Grate cucumber or put through food chopper, using fine blade; drain. Measure ½ cup drained grated cucumber.

Blend one 8-ounce package cream cheese, softened and ¼ cup mayonnaise or salad dressing. Stir in one 13½-ounce can crushed pineapple, undrained, the grated cucumber, 2 tablespoons minced onion, and ½ teaspoon grated lemon peel; mix well. Stir in remaining gelatin mixture. Chill till partially set. Pour over set gelatin in mold. Chill firm. Serves 8.

ROSY STRAWBERRY RING

- 2 3-ounce packages strawberry-flavored gelatin
- 2 cups boiling water
- 2 10-ounce packages frozen sliced strawberries
- 1 13½-ounce can (1½ cups) crushed pineapple
- 2 large fully ripe bananas, finely diced
- 2 tablespoons lemon juice
  Sour-cream Dressing

Dissolve gelatin in water. Add berries, stirring occasionally until thawed. Stir in pineapple, banana, and lemon juice. Pour into 6½-cup mold. Chill firm, 5 to 6 hours. Pass *Sour-cream Dressing:* Combine 1 cup dairy sour cream, 1 teaspoon sugar, ¼ teaspoon ground ginger, and dash salt. Chill. Serves 8.

MOLDED CIDER WALDORF

4 cups apple cider
2 3-ounce packages pineapple-
  grapefruit-flavored gelatin
1 teaspoon salt
2 tart medium apples
½ cup diced celery
½ cup coarsely broken California
  walnuts

Bring *2 cups* of the cider to boiling; add gelatin and salt; stir to dissolve gelatin. Add remaining cider. Pour *1 cup* of the gelatin mixture into a 5-cup melon mold; chill both portions of gelatin till *partially* set. Cut half of one apple (unpared) in thin wedges. Following the lines of the mold, arrange apple wedges in gelatin. Chill till almost firm.

Meanwhile, pare and dice remaining apples; fold diced apple, celery, and nuts into remaining gelatin. Spoon over gelatin in mold. Chill till firm. Makes 8 to 10 servings.

SPICED PEACH MOLD

1 8½-ounce can pineapple slices
1 1 pound 13-ounce jar spiced
  peaches
2 3-ounce packages orange-
  pineapple-flavored gelatin
  • • •
2 tablespoons lemon juice
¼ teaspoon salt
2 7-ounce bottles (about 2 cups)
  ginger ale, chilled

Drain and halve pineapple slices. Drain peaches, reserving syrup. Remove pits. Add water to syrup to make 2 cups. In a saucepan, combine peach syrup mixture and gelatin; heat and stir till gelatin dissolves. Add lemon juice and salt. Chill till cold but not set.

Pour ginger ale carefully into gelatin; stir with up-and-down motion. Pour about *half* the gelatin into 6½-cup ring mold; chill both portions of gelatin till partially set.

Arrange most of the peaches and pineapple around the mold, gently placing the fruits in the gelatin. Chill till almost firm. Cut any remaining peaches and pineapple and fold into reserved gelatin. Pour carefully over gelatin and fruit in mold. Chill till set. Unmold on greens. Makes 8 to 10 servings.

JUBILEE SALAD MOLD

1 10-ounce package frozen
  raspberries, thawed
½ cup currant jelly
2 cups water
2 3-ounce packages red raspberry-
  flavored gelatin
½ cup sherry
¼ cup lemon juice
1 1-pound can (2 cups) pitted dark
  sweet cherries, drained

Drain raspberries, reserving the syrup. Combine jelly and ½ *cup of the water;* heat and stir till jelly melts. Add remaining 1½ cups water and the gelatin; heat and stir till gelatin dissolves. Remove from heat; add sherry, lemon juice, and reserved raspberry syrup. Chill till *partially set.* Fold raspberries and cherries into gelatin. Pour into 6-cup mold. Chill till firm. Makes 8 servings.

RED RASPBERRY SALAD

2 10-ounce packages frozen
  raspberries, thawed
2 3-ounce packages red raspberry-
  flavored gelatin
1 1-pound can (2 cups) applesauce

Drain raspberries, reserving 1 cup syrup. Dissolve gelatin in 2 cups boiling water; stir in reserved syrup and applesauce. Chill till partially set; fold in raspberries. Pour into 6-cup ring mold; chill firm. Serves 6 to 8.

CRANBERRY WALDORF MOLD

1 pint bottle (2 cups) cranberry-
  juice cocktail
1 3-ounce package lemon-flavored
  gelatin
¼ teaspoon salt
1 cup diced unpared apple
½ cup chopped celery
¼ cup broken California walnuts

Heat *1 cup* cranberry-juice cocktail just to boiling. Dissolve gelatin in it. Add remaining juice and the salt. Chill till partially set. Stir in apple, celery, and nuts. Pour into 4 to 6 individual molds. Chill firm. Serves 4 to 6.

HARVEST FRUIT MOLD

In saucepan, combine one 11-ounce package mixed dried fruits with water to cover. Simmer gently, covered, 25 to 30 minutes, adding ⅓ cup sugar last 5 minutes of cooking. Drain fruit, reserving syrup; add water to make 2 cups. Dissolve two 3-ounce packages orange-flavored gelatin in 2 cups boiling water; stir in syrup. Chill till partially set.

Pit prunes; cut up all fruit; fold into gelatin. Pour into 6-cup ring mold. Chill till firm. Unmold on platter and garnish with additional cooked dried fruit and greens, if desired. Makes 8 servings.

OFF WITH THE MOLD!

To unmold gelatin, loosen edge (and around center of ring mold) with tip of knife. Invert mold on platter. Dip a towel in warm water; wring out; lay on top of mold for a few seconds. Lift mold straight up. Chill till serving time.

Or loosen edge of mold as above. Dip mold just to rim in *warm* water for few seconds. Tilt mold slightly; ease gelatin away from one side to let air in. Then tilt and rotate mold so air can loosen gelatin all the way around. Put chilled serving plate upside down over mold; holding plate and mold together, invert and lift off mold. If serving plate is slightly wet, gelatin can be positioned on plate after removing mold.

When using a mold with an intricate design, brush inside lightly but thoroughly with salad oil; omit dipping in warm water when unmolding the salad.

If mold is high or must stand out on warm day, omit small amount of liquid.

CINNAMON SALAD

  ¼ cup red cinnamon candies
  1 3-ounce package lemon-flavored gelatin
1½ cups boiling water
  1 cup applesauce
  1 3-ounce package cream cheese, softened
  2 tablespoons milk
  1 tablespoon mayonnaise
  ¼ teaspoon salt

Dissolve candies and gelatin in boiling water. Chill till partially set. Fold in applesauce. Turn into 10x6x1½-inch dish; chill firm. Cream remaining ingredients; spread over gelatin. Chill. Cut in squares. Serves 8.

GRAPEFRUIT-SHERBET RING

  2 1-pound cans grapefruit sections
  2 3-ounce packages lime-flavored gelatin
  1 pint lime sherbet
  ½ cup broken pecans

Drain and dice grapefruit, reserving syrup. Add enough water to syrup to make 2 cups. Add gelatin; heat and stir till gelatin is dissolved. Stir in sherbet; chill till partially set. Fold in fruit and nuts; turn into 6-cup ring mold. Chill till set. Serves 8 to 10.

TANGERINE-APRICOT MOLD

  2 envelopes unflavored gelatin
  ½ cup sugar
    Dash salt
1¾ cups tangerine juice*
  1 12-ounce can (1½ cups) apricot nectar
  3 egg whites
  ½ cup whipping cream, whipped

Combine first 4 ingredients. Cook and stir over medium heat till gelatin dissolves. Stir in apricot nectar; chill till partially set. Add egg whites; beat till fluffy. Chill till partially set; fold in whipped cream. Pile into 6-cup mold; chill firm. Serves 8 to 10.

*Reconstitute one 6-ounce can frozen tangerine juice concentrate; measure 1¾ cups.

PEACH-CHERRY SPARKLE

    1 1-pound can (2 cups) pitted dark
      sweet cherries
    ½ cup sugar
    2 envelopes (2 tablespoons)
      unflavored gelatin
    ½ teaspoon salt
    ½ cup lemon juice
    2 7-ounce bottles ginger ale
      (about 2 cups)
    1 1-pound can sliced peaches,
      drained and diced (1¼ cups)

Drain cherries, reserving syrup; add water to syrup to make 1¼ cups. In saucepan, combine sugar, gelatin, and salt; stir in syrup. Cook and stir over medium heat till gelatin dissolves. Remove from heat; add lemon juice.

Allow to cool but not set. Resting bottle on rim of pan, gradually pour in ginger ale, stirring gently with up-and-down motion. Chill till partially set. Fold in cherries and peaches. Turn into 6-cup ring mold. Chill till firm, 6 hours or overnight. Serves 8 to 10.

ORANGE APRICOT RING

    2 1-pound cans (4 cups) apricot
      halves
    2 3-ounce packages orange-
      flavored gelatin
      Dash salt
    1 6-ounce can frozen orange juice
      concentrate
    2 tablespoons lemon juice
    1 7-ounce bottle (about 1 cup)
      lemon-lime carbonated beverage

Drain apricots; reserve 1½ cups syrup. Puree apricots in blender or put through sieve to make 2 cups puree. Combine reserved syrup, gelatin, and salt; heat to boiling; stir to dissolve gelatin. Remove from heat.

Add apricot puree, orange concentrate, and lemon juice; stir to melt concentrate. Slowly pour carbonated beverage down side of pan; mix gently with up-and-down motion. Pour into 6½-cup ring mold. Chill till firm, about 6 hours or overnight. Unmold. Fill center with lettuce leaves; arrange fresh or canned fruits around salad. Pass mayonnaise which has been folded into an equal amount of whipping cream, whipped. Serves 10 to 12.

SPARKLING HONEYDEW LOAF

Sour cream and mayonnaise form built-in dressing—

    2 envelopes (2 tablespoons)
      unflavored gelatin
    1 6-ounce can frozen lemonade
      concentrate, thawed
    1 7-ounce bottle (about 1 cup)
      ginger ale
    2 tablespoons maraschino cherry
      juice
    ½ medium honeydew melon, cut in
      ½-inch cubes (2 cups)
    ¼ cup sliced maraschino cherries
    ¼ cup dairy sour cream
    ¼ cup mayonnaise or salad dressing

Soften gelatin in ½ cup cold water. Add 1¾ cups boiling water; stir till gelatin dissolves. Stir in thawed concentrate. Gently stir in ginger ale. Divide gelatin mixture in half.

Stir cherry juice into first half. Chill till partially set; fold in fruits. Turn into 8½x4½x 2½-inch baking dish; chill.

Add sour cream and mayonnaise to remaining gelatin. Beat with rotary beater till smooth. Leave at room temperature till fruit layer is almost set. Slowly pour sour cream gelatin over fruit layer. Chill 3 to 4 hours, or until firm. Makes 8 to 10 servings.

SUNSHINE CITRUS CUPS

    1 8¾-ounce can (1 cup) crushed
      pineapple
    1 1-pound can (2 cups) grapefruit
      sections
    ¼ cup sugar
    2 envelopes (2 tablespoons)
      unflavored gelatin
      Dash salt
    ⅓ cup broken California walnuts
    2 7-ounce bottles (about 2 cups)
      ginger ale, *well chilled*

Drain fruits; reserve syrups. Combine sugar, gelatin, salt, and reserved syrups; cook and stir over low heat till gelatin dissolves. Chill till cold but still liquid; stir in the fruits and nuts. Carefully pour ginger ale down side of bowl; stir gently with up-and-down motion. Chill till partially set. Turn into 8 individual molds; chill till firm.

ORANGE-APRICOT FREEZE

Looks and tastes like orange sherbet!

2 8-ounce cartons (2 cups) orange-
  flavored yogurt
1 1-pound 1-ounce can apricot
  halves
½ cup sugar
⅓ cup coarsely chopped pecans

Stir yogurt in carton to blend. Drain apricots; cut up fruit. Combine yogurt, apricots, sugar, and nuts. Line muffin pan with 12 paper bake cups. Spoon yogurt mixture into cups. Freeze till firm, about 2 hours. Remove bake cups from salads; let stand at room temperature a few minutes before serving. Serves 12.

FROZEN CRANBERRY SALADS

Whip 1 cup whipping cream with ¼ cup sugar and dash salt to soft peaks. Stir in 2 tablespoons mayonnaise or salad dressing, mixing well. Fold in one 1-pound can (2 cups) whole cranberry sauce, diced, and one-half 6-ounce can (⅓ cup) frozen orange juice concentrate, thawed. Line muffin pans with foil or paper bake cups; fill with mixture.

Freeze till firm. Remove bake cups; let salads stand at room temperature 10 minutes before serving. Makes 6 to 8 servings.

DATE SOUFFLE SALADS

1 8-ounce package cream cheese,
  softened
¼ cup maple syrup
1 tablespoon lemon juice
1 medium banana, mashed (½ cup)
1 8¾-ounce can (1 cup) crushed
  pineapple, drained
½ cup finely chopped dates
½ cup chopped pecans
1 cup whipping cream, whipped

Cream the cheese; beat in syrup, lemon juice and mashed banana. Stir in pineapple, dates, and pecans. Fold in whipped cream. Line 6 to 8 muffin cups with paper bake cups; fill with salad. Freeze till firm. Remove bake cups. Let salads stand 15 minutes at room temperature before serving. Serves 6 to 8.

FROSTED FRUIT SLICES

2 3-ounce packages cream cheese
1 cup mayonnaise
1 1-pound 14-ounce can (3½ cups)
  fruit cocktail, well drained
½ cup drained maraschino cherries,
  quartered
2½ cups miniature marshmallows *or*
  24 regular marshmallows, cut up
1 cup whipping cream, whipped

Soften the cream cheese; blend with mayonnaise. Stir in fruit cocktail, maraschino cherries, and marshmallows. Fold in whipped cream. Tint pale pink with few drops red food coloring or maraschino cherry juice.

Pour into two 1-quart round ice cream or freezer containers or two No. 2½ cans or refrigerator trays. Freeze firm about 6 hours or overnight. To serve, cut bottom from container or can; let stand at room temperature a few minutes; slide salad out and slice. Or, cut in squares or wedges from refrigerator tray. Makes 10 to 12 servings.

FROSTED FRUIT MOLD

1 8-ounce package cream cheese,
  softened
¼ cup mayonnaise or salad dressing
¼ cup confectioners' sugar
2 tablespoons lemon juice
½ teaspoon vanilla

• • •

1 1-pound 4½-ounce can pineapple
  tidbits, drained (1½ cups)
1 10-ounce package frozen blueberries, thawed and drained
1 12-ounce package frozen peaches,
  thawed, drained, and diced
2 cups miniature marshmallows
1 cup whipping cream
  Few drops green food coloring

Combine cream cheese, mayonnaise, confectioners' sugar, lemon juice, and vanilla. Beat till smooth. Fold in pineapple, blueberries, peaches, and marshmallows. Whip cream; add coloring to tint a delicate green. Fold cream into fruit mixture. Turn into 5-cup melon mold and freeze. To serve, allow melon mold to stand at room temperature 20 to 30 minutes before serving. Makes 12 servings.

STRAWBERRY FREEZE

   1 8¾-ounce can (1 cup) crushed
      pineapple, drained
   1 cup strawberries, crushed
   ⅓ cup sugar
   1 cup cream-style cottage cheese
   2 teaspoons lemon juice
   ½ cup whipping cream, whipped

Combine pineapple, strawberries, and sugar;
mix well. Combine cheese and lemon juice;
beat smooth with rotary or electric beater.
Fold in whipped cream and fruit mixture;
turn into 1-quart refrigerator tray; freeze
firm, about 2 hours. To serve, let stand at
room temperature 15 minutes. Serves 5 or 6.

**Dark sweet cherries and golden apricots
accent creamy-rich Frosty Salad Loaf.**

AVOCADO FRUIT FREEZE

Creamy salad with blend of avocado and pear—

   1 large avocado
   2 tablespoons lemon juice
   1 3-ounce package cream cheese,
      softened
   2 tablespoons sugar
   ¼ cup mayonnaise or salad dressing
   ¼ teaspoon salt
   1 1-pound can pears, drained and
      diced (1½ cups)
   ¼ cup well drained, chopped
      maraschino cherries
   ½ cup whipping cream, whipped

Halve, peel, and dice avocado; sprinkle with
1 tablespoon of the lemon juice. Blend cream
cheese, remaining lemon juice, sugar, mayonnaise, and salt. Add diced avocado, pears,
and chopped cherries; fold in whipped cream.
Pour into 3-cup refrigerator tray; freeze till
firm, about 6 hours or overnight.

    Let stand at room temperature about 15
minutes before serving. Garnish with kabobs
of maraschino cherries and avocado balls
(made with melon baller). Makes 6 servings.

FROSTY SALAD LOAF

    1 8-ounce package cream cheese
    1 cup dairy sour cream
    ¼ cup sugar
    ¼ teaspoon salt
  1½ cups pitted, halved fresh
       dark sweet cherries
    1 1-pound can (2 cups) apricot
       halves, drained and sliced
    1 8¾-ounce can (1 cup) crushed
       pineapple, drained
    2 cups miniature marshmallows
       Few drops red food coloring

Let cream cheese stand at room temperature
to soften, then beat fluffy. Stir in sour cream,
sugar, and salt, then fruits and marshmallows.
Add few drops red food coloring to tint pale
pink. Pour into an 8½x4½x2½-inch loaf
pan. Freeze about 6 hours or overnight.

    To serve let stand out a few minutes, then
remove from container, slice and place on
crisp greens. Trim with pitted cherries and
peach slices. Makes 8 servings.

Dressings: sweet or sassy

POPPY SEED LIME DRESSING

⅓ cup vinegar
¼ cup lime juice
¾ cup sugar
1 teaspoon salt
1 teaspoon dry mustard
1 teaspoon poppy seed
1 teaspoon paprika
1 cup salad oil
½ teaspoon onion juice

Heat vinegar and lime juice to boiling. Combine dry ingredients; add to hot mixture. Stir to dissolve sugar. Add oil and onion juice. Beat with rotary beater till thoroughly mixed and slightly thickened. Chill. Serve on canned or fresh fruit. Makes 1¾ cups.

HONEY-LIME DRESSING

1 beaten egg
¼ cup lime juice
½ cup honey
Dash *each* salt and ground mace
1 cup dairy sour cream

Combine egg, lime juice, and honey; cook and stir over low heat till mixture thickens. Stir in dash salt and mace. Cool. Fold in sour cream. Chill. Makes 1½ cups dressing.

FLUFFY CITRUS DRESSING

In saucepan, beat 1 egg; add ½ cup sugar, 1 tablespoon grated orange peel, 2 teaspoons grated lemon peel, and 2 tablespoons lemon juice. Cook and stir over low heat till thick, about 5 minutes; cool thoroughly. Fold in 1 cup whipping cream, whipped. Chill. Makes about 2⅓ cups dressing.

ORANGE CHUTNEY DRESSING

In screw top jar, combine 1 cup sweet French salad dressing, 1 teaspoon grated orange peel, and 2 tablespoons finely chopped chutney. Cover; shake. Chill. Makes 1 cup.

RUBY SALAD DRESSING

1 3-ounce package cream cheese
2 tablespoons milk
1 tablespoon lemon juice
¼ cup currant jelly
Few drops red food coloring
½ cup whipping cream, whipped

Soften cream cheese; beat with milk, lemon juice, and dash salt. Beat in jelly and food coloring. Chill. Fold in the whipped cream. Makes 1½ cups dressing.

BANANA CREAM DRESSING

3 fully ripe bananas, peeled
2 tablespoons brown sugar
2 tablespoons honey
1 cup whipping cream, whipped

Mash together bananas, sugar, and honey till smooth; sieve. Fold banana mixture into whipped cream. (Or fold banana mixture into prepared topping—use one 2-ounce package dessert topping mix.) Makes 3 cups.

WALNUT-RUM DRESSING

1½ cups mayonnaise
¼ cup light rum
2 tablespoons red raspberry syrup
¼ cup finely chopped walnuts
Dash cayenne
1 cup whipping cream, whipped

Blend first 5 ingredients well. Fold into cream. Pile into serving dish; sprinkle with additional nuts. Makes 2¾ cups.

ORANGE FRENCH DRESSING

Combine in a jar, ⅓ cup frozen orange juice concentrate, thawed, ⅔ cup salad oil, 1 tablespoon vinegar, ¼ cup sugar, ¼ teaspoon salt, ¼ teaspoon dry mustard, and dash bottled hot pepper sauce; cover and shake till well mixed. Chill. Makes about 1⅛ cups.

To dress up a fresh fruit plate, serve luscious pink Cherry Cream Dressing. With oven-hot quick breads, you will have a light luncheon.

GINGER-HONEY DRESSING

Combine 6 tablespoons honey, 3 tablespoons lemon or lime juice, and 1 teaspoon ground ginger *or* finely chopped candied ginger; mix. Chill. Makes ½ cup dressing.

CURRY CREAM DRESSING

Combine 1 cup dairy sour cream, ¼ teaspoon curry powder, and 2 teaspoons finely chopped candied ginger; chill. Makes 1 cup.

LEMON MAYONNAISE

Blend ½ cup mayonnaise or salad dressing and ¼ cup frozen lemonade concentrate, thawed. Fold in ½ cup whipping cream, whipped. Makes about 1½ cups dressing.

CHERRY CREAM DRESSING

1 3-ounce package cream cheese, softened
2 tablespoons mayonnaise
2 tablespoons maraschino cherry juice
1 tablespoon milk
2 teaspoons lemon juice
Few drops red food coloring
1 2-ounce package dessert topping mix
1 tablespoon finely chopped maraschino cherries

Combine first 6 ingredients; beat till smooth. Prepare topping mix according to package directions; fold into cheese mixture. Stir in cherries. Chill. To serve, whip till fluffy; pile into bowl. Drop one drop red food coloring atop; swirl in. Makes about 1⅓ cups.

BREADS
AND
SANDWICHES

*Warm yeast breads from oven
to shelf above
include Crown Coffee Bread
and Petal Bread,
made from the same dough.
Quick bread on
shelf below is Apricot Crescent.*

Oven-fresh yeast breads

BASIC FRUIT DOUGH

  2 packages active dry yeast
  ½ cup warm water
  ¾ cup unsweetened pineapple juice
  ⅓ cup sugar
  1½ teaspoons salt
  ½ cup shortening
  2 teaspoons grated lemon peel
  4½ to 5 cups sifted all-purpose flour
  2 eggs
  ¾ cup light raisins
  ½ cup chopped candied pineapple

Soften yeast in water; set aside. Heat juice; combine with sugar, salt, and shortening. Stir till shortening melts and sugar dissolves; cool to lukewarm. Stir in peel and 1½ *cups* of the flour; beat well. Add eggs, softened yeast, and fruits. Beat. Add enough remaining flour to make soft to moderately stiff dough. Turn out on lightly floured surface; knead till smooth, about 10 minutes. Place in greased bowl; turn once to grease surface. Cover; let rise in warm place till doubled, 1 to 1½ hours. Punch down; let rest 10 minutes.

Shape dough in one of the following ways:

CROWN COFFEE BREAD

Using Basic Fruit Dough, pat ¾ of dough evenly into a greased 10-inch tube pan. Divide remaining dough in half; roll each to 28-inch strand. Twist together; place on top of dough; seal ends. Cover, let rise till doubled, 45 to 60 minutes. Bake at 375° about 45 minutes. Brush with butter or margarine when it comes from oven and sprinkle lightly with sugar. Makes 1 large loaf.

TOPKNOT LOAVES

Using Basic Fruit Dough, divide dough in fourths; pat into 4 well-greased 1-pound cans; smooth tops. Cover; let rise till dough is about 1-inch above top of can, 30 to 45 minutes. Bake at 375° about 40 minutes. Remove from cans; cool. Frost with Confectioners' Sugar Icing; top with nuts. Makes 4 loaves.

PETAL BREAD

Using Basic Fruit Dough, divide dough in thirds. Shape each into a smooth ball. Place balls on lightly greased baking sheet with balls just touching. Cover and let rise till doubled, about 45 minutes. Bake at 350° about 35 minutes. Cool. Prepare *Confectioners' Sugar Icing:* Combine ¾ cup sifted confectioners' sugar and 1 tablespoon milk; spread over bread. Trim with almonds and candied cherries. Makes one 3-part loaf.

HOT CROSS ROLLS

Using Basic Fruit Dough, turn dough out on lightly floured surface. Roll to ½ inch thick. Cut with 2½-inch biscuit cutter and shape in rolls. Place on greased baking sheet; cover; let rise till almost doubled, about 45 minutes. Cut shallow cross in each roll with sharp knife. Brush tops with 1 slightly beaten egg white. Bake at 375° about 15 minutes. Cool slightly. Mark crosses on rolls with Confectioners' Sugar Icing. Makes 2 dozen.

RAISIN-NUT SWIRL LOAF

  1 package active dry yeast
  1 egg
  1 tablespoon granulated sugar
  2½ cups packaged biscuit mix
  2 tablespoons butter, softened
  2 tablespoons brown sugar
  ½ cup chopped California walnuts
  ½ cup raisins

Soften yeast in ½ cup warm water; set aside. Stir in next 3 ingredients. Beat vigorously; knead on lightly floured surface till smooth. Roll in 15x8-inch rectangle ¼ inch thick. Butter; sprinkle with remaining ingredients. Roll up from narrow side; seal edges. Place seam side down in greased 8½x4½x2½-inch loaf dish. Cover; let rise in warm place till nearly doubled, about 1 hour. Bake at 375° about 25 minutes. Cover with foil after 20 minutes. Cool. Frost; sprinkle additional nuts and raisins over top. Makes 1 loaf.

Frosted Orange Crescents are just right to serve at a midmorning brunch with scrambled eggs, mushroom crowns, and grilled sausages.

ORANGE CRESCENTS

Soften 1 package active dry yeast in ¼ cup warm water. Combine ¾ cup scalded milk, ¼ cup shortening, ¼ cup sugar, and 1 teaspoon salt; cool to lukewarm. Add 1 cup sifted all-purpose flour; beat well. Beat in yeast mixture, 1 egg, and 1 teaspoon shredded orange peel. Add 2 cups sifted all-purpose flour; mix well. Place in greased bowl; turn to grease surface. Cover; refrigerate at least 2 hours. Divide in 2 parts. Roll each to 9-inch circle. Cut each in 12 wedges. Starting at wide end, roll up each wedge. Place, points down, on greased baking sheets. Let rise in warm place till doubled, about 1¼ hours. Bake at 375° for 10 to 12 minutes. While warm, spread with *Glaze:* Combine 1½ cups sifted confectioners' sugar, ½ teaspoon grated orange peel, dash salt, and orange juice for desired consistency. Makes 24.

LEMON-SPICE PUFFS

    1 package active dry yeast
    ¾ cup milk, scalded
    6 tablespoons sugar
    ⅓ cup shortening
    1 teaspoon salt
    1 tablespoon grated lemon peel
    1 teaspoon lemon juice
    2 beaten eggs
    3 cups sifted all-purpose flour

Soften yeast in ¼ cup warm water. To milk add next 5 ingredients. Cool to lukewarm. Add eggs and yeast. Add flour, 1 cup at a time, beating till smooth. Cover; let rise till doubled. Stir down dough. Fill greased muffin pans half full. Combine 1 tablespoon sugar and 1 teaspoon ground cinnamon; sprinkle over rolls. Cover; let rise till doubled. Bake at 375° about 20 minutes. Makes 18.

ORANGE COFFEE BRAID

　2　packages active dry yeast
　¼　cup warm water
　1　cup milk, scalded
　⅓　cup frozen orange juice
　　　concentrate, thawed
　1　teaspoon shredded lemon peel
　1　egg
　½　cup sugar
　½　teaspoon salt
　5　to 5½ cups sifted all-purpose
　　　flour
　6　tablespoons butter or margarine,
　　　softened

　　　• • •

　¾　cup sifted confectioners' sugar
　1　tablespoon frozen orange juice
　　　concentrate, thawed
　　　Toasted slivered almonds

Soften yeast in warm water. Cool milk to luke-warm. Add milk to yeast mixture with ⅓ cup thawed orange juice concentrate and peel. Add egg, sugar, salt, and 2½ *cups* of the flour. Beat well. Blend in butter or margarine. Add enough of the remaining flour to make a soft dough. Turn out on lightly floured surface and knead till smooth, about 8 to 10 minutes. Place in greased bowl, turning once to grease surface. Cover and let rise in a warm place till doubled, about 1½ hours. Punch down; divide in half and let rest about 10 minutes.

From one half of dough, cut off one third and set aside. Divide remaining two thirds into three equal portions. Roll each portion to 12-inch strand. Place strands on greased baking sheet and braid.

Divide reserved one third of dough into three equal portions and roll each portion into 12-inch strand. Braid and place atop first braid. Repeat with other half of dough, forming two braids. Cover; let rise till almost doubled, about 45 minutes. Bake in a moderate oven (350°) for 30 to 35 minutes.

Beat together the confectioners' sugar, 1 tablespoon thawed orange juice concentrate, and 1 tablespoon water. Brush over tops of braids when they come from the oven. Sprinkle tops with almonds. Makes 2 braids.

← Orange Coffee Braid is the best excuse for a coffee break. Serve one braid warm from the oven; freeze other for later use.

SPECIAL OCCASION BREAD

　1　package active dry yeast
　3　tablespoons sugar
　3　egg yolks
　½　cup milk
　4　cups sifted all-purpose flour
　1　teaspoon salt
　1　cup shortening
　¾　cup sugar
　1½　teaspoons ground cinnamon
　3　stiffly beaten egg whites
　1½　cups chopped dates
　1　cup chopped nuts

Soften yeast in ½ cup warm water; stir in 3 tablespoons sugar. Combine egg yolks and milk. Sift flour and salt together; cut in shortening till like coarse crumbs. Stir in yeast and egg yolk mixtures; mix well. Form into ball; place in greased bowl, turning once to grease surface; cover; chill overnight. Divide dough into 3 parts. On lightly floured surface, roll each into 15x8-inch rectangle. Stir the ¾ cup sugar and cinnamon into egg whites. Spread ⅓ over each rectangle, leaving ½ inch around edge. Sprinkle each with ⅓ of the dates and nuts. Starting with long side of dough, roll as for jelly roll, seal edges and ends. Place on greased baking sheet; form into crescent shape. Let rise till doubled, about 45 to 50 minutes. Bake at 350° about 25 minutes. Glaze with confectioners' icing while hot. Decorate with nuts or candied fruits, if desired. Makes 3 crescent-shaped loaves.

DATE-JAM BRAID

Dissolve 1 package active dry yeast in ½ cup warm water. Add 1 slightly beaten egg, 1 tablespoon sugar, and 2½ cups packaged biscuit mix. Beat till smooth. Turn out on lightly floured surface; knead 10 to 15 strokes. Roll to 9-inch square. Place on greased baking sheet. Combine ½ cup raspberry jam, ½ cup snipped dates, and ½ cup chopped California walnuts. Spread mixture down center ⅓ of dough. Cut dough on each side of filling in 1½-inch crosswise strips. Lap strips of dough over filling in crisscross pattern. Let rise in warm place about 45 minutes. Bake at 350° about 20 minutes, or till golden. Brush with melted butter; sprinkle with sugar. Serve warm or cool. Makes 1 braid.

JEWEL-TOP STAR BREAD

1 package active dry yeast
¼ cup warm water
¼ cup milk
3 tablespoons shortening
3 tablespoons sugar
½ teaspoon salt
1 teaspoon grated lemon peel
1 egg
1½ cups sifted all-purpose flour
1 tablespoon butter, melted
2 tablespoons brown sugar
1 tablespoon light corn syrup
   Candied pineapple and cherries

Soften yeast in water. Heat milk and shortening till shortening melts. Stir in next 3 ingredients. Cool to lukewarm. Add egg and softened yeast. Add flour, ½ cup at a time, beating smooth after each addition. Cover; let rise till doubled. Stir down dough. Combine butter, brown sugar, and corn syrup; spread in bottom of 5-cup star mold. Arrange candied fruit in bottom of mold to form pattern. Spoon dough carefully over fruit. Cover; let rise till doubled. Bake at 375° for 20 to 25 minutes. Cool 1 minute. Loosen sides and turn out onto rack. Cool.

CHERRY PUFF ROLLS

Soften 1 package active dry yeast in ¼ cup warm water. Combine ⅔ cup scalded milk, ¼ cup sugar, 3 tablespoons butter, and 1 teaspoon salt; stir to dissolve; cool to lukewarm. Add yeast, 1 egg, and 1 cup sifted all-purpose flour; beat smooth. Add 2¼ to 2¾ cups sifted all-purpose flour to make soft dough.

Knead on floured surface till smooth, 8 to 10 minutes. Place in greased bowl; turn once to grease surface. Cover; let rise till doubled, 1½ to 2 hours. Punch down; let rest 10 minutes. Roll ½ inch thick on floured surface. Spread with 2 tablespoons softened butter; fold in half, pinch edges together. Roll ½ inch thick; spread with 2 tablespoons softened butter; fold, seal, and roll again.

Cut in 2½-inch circles; place on greased baking sheet. Cover; let double, 20 to 30 minutes. Make depression in center of each; fill with cherry preserves. Bake at 400° about 10 to 12 minutes. While warm, frost with Confectioners' Sugar Icing. Makes 12 rolls.

PRUNE-NUT BRAID

1 13¾-ounce package hot roll mix
2 tablespoons butter or margarine, melted and cooled
1 teaspoon grated orange peel
¾ cup canned prune filling
¼ cup chopped pecans

Prepare hot roll mix according to package directions; add butter and peel; mix well. Cover; let rise in warm place till doubled, about 1 hour. On lightly floured surface, knead dough about 1 minute. Roll dough to a 12-inch square. Cut into 3 strips.

Spread ¼ cup prune filling down center of each strip. Sprinkle evenly with nuts. Pinch dough up around filling to form 3 ropes. Place on greased baking sheet and braid dough; pinch ends together. Cover and let rise till almost doubled, about 40 minutes. Bake in moderate oven (375°) about 25 minutes or till done. Glaze while warm and decorate with red sugar and pecan halves. Serve warm. Makes 1 large braid.

ORANGE DOUGHNUTS

1 package active dry yeast
¼ cup warm water
2 teaspoons grated orange peel
¾ cup warm orange juice
¼ cup butter, melted
½ cup sugar
¾ teaspoon salt

· · ·

4 to 4½ cups sifted all-purpose flour
1 egg

Soften yeast in warm water. Combine next 5 ingredients. Add 1 cup flour; beat well. Beat in softened yeast and egg. Add enough remaining flour to make soft dough. Turn out on lightly floured surface; knead till smooth, about 5 to 7 minutes. Place in greased bowl, turning once to grease surface. Chill dough thoroughly, about 1½ to 2 hours.

Roll out on lightly floured surface to ½ inch thick. Cut with 2½-inch doughnut cutter. Let rise till light, about 1¼ hours. Fry in deep hot fat (375°) till browned. Drain thoroughly; dust with confectioners' sugar. Makes about 1½ dozen doughnuts.

Easy holiday yeast breads include no-knead
Jewel-top Star Bread and Prune-nut Braid
that gets a fast start from a hot roll mix.

CHERRY BREAD

- 1 package active dry yeast
- ½ cup warm water

  . . .

- ½ cup milk
- ¼ cup shortening
- ¼ cup sugar
- 1 teaspoon salt
- 3 cups sifted all-purpose flour
- 1 egg

  . . .

- ¼ cup finely chopped maraschino cherries
- ½ cup flaked coconut
- 2 tablespoons sugar
  Confectioners' sugar icing

Soften yeast in water. Scald milk; add shortening and stir till melted. Stir in ¼ cup sugar and salt. Cool to lukewarm.

Add 1½ cups flour. Mix well. Add softened yeast and egg. Beat well. Add enough of the remaining flour to make a soft dough. Turn out on lightly floured surface and knead till smooth and satiny, about 2½ minutes. Place in greased bowl, turning once to grease surface. Cover and let rise in warm place till doubled, about 1½ hours.

When dough is light, punch down. Let rest 10 minutes. Divide dough in half. Roll half into a 12x6-inch rectangle. Combine chopped cherries, coconut, and 2 tablespoons sugar. Spread *half* the mixture over rectangle. Beginning at short side, roll up as for jelly roll; seal edges and ends. Repeat with remaining half of dough and cherry mixture.

Place in 2 greased 7½x3¾x2¼-inch loaf pans. Let rise till doubled. Bake in moderate oven (350°) about 35 to 40 minutes. Remove from pans. While warm, frost with Confectioners' Sugar Icing. Makes 2 loaves.

Quick bread treats

APRICOT CRESCENT

   2 cups sifted all-purpose flour
   1 tablespoon sugar
   1 tablespoon baking powder
   1 teaspoon salt
   ¼ cup shortening
   2 eggs
     Milk
   1 tablespoon melted butter
     Apricot Filling

Sift together dry ingredients. Cut in shortening till mixture is crumbly. Beat together 1 whole egg and 1 egg yolk, reserving remaining egg white. Add enough milk to egg to make ⅔ cup; add to dry ingredients and stir only till moistened. Turn out on lightly floured surface and knead gently 30 seconds. Roll to 14x9-inch rectangle. Brush with melted butter; spread with Apricot Filling. Roll up like jelly roll starting with long side; seal edge well. Place, sealed edge down, on greased baking sheet and curve into crescent shape. With scissors, cut 1-inch slices to within ¼ inch of the inner edge. Turn each slice slightly on its side. Beat reserved egg white lightly and brush over dough; sprinkle with sugar. Bake at 425° for 15 to 20 minutes.

Apricot Filling: Combine in heavy saucepan 1 cup chopped dried apricots, ¼ cup raisins, ½ cup sugar, and ¾ cup water. Boil until thick, about 10 minutes; stirring frequently. Add 1 teaspoon lemon juice; mix well. Cool partially. Makes 1 coffeecake.

CRANBERRY COFFEECAKE

Sift together 1½ cups sifted all-purpose flour, ½ cup sugar, 2 teaspoons baking powder, 1 teaspoon salt, and ½ teaspoon soda. Stir in ½ cup chopped walnuts. Combine 1 ripe banana, mashed (½ cup), ½ cup milk, 1 beaten egg, and ¼ cup melted shortening. Add to flour mixture; stir to blend. Pour into greased 9x9x2-inch baking pan. Cut one 8-ounce can jellied cranberry sauce into 4 slices; quarter each. Arrange atop batter; top each with a pecan half. Sprinkle ¼ cup sugar over all. Bake at 400° for 25 to 30 minutes.

CITRUS COFFEECAKE

   2 tablespoons butter or margarine
   1 tablespoon frozen orange juice
     concentrate, thawed
   1 teaspoon lemon juice
   ⅓ cup sugar
   ¼ teaspoon ground cinnamon
   ¼ cup coarsely chopped pecans
   1 8-ounce package refrigerated
     buttermilk biscuits

Melt butter in 8x1½-inch round cake pan. Stir in orange juice concentrate, lemon juice, sugar, cinnamon, and nuts. Top with refrigerated biscuits. Bake in moderate oven (350°) 25 minutes. Cool 1 minute; invert on serving plate. Serve warm. Makes 1 coffeecake.

SPICY PEAR COFFEECAKE

Get a head start and use a spice cake mix—then just add the topping and serve while still warm—

   1 9-inch square spice cake
   3 fresh ripe pears
   ⅓ cup granulated sugar
   ⅓ cup water
   2 tablespoons red cinnamon candies
   • • •
   6 tablespoons butter or margarine,
     melted
   ¾ cup brown sugar
   ⅓ cup chopped California walnuts
     Dash salt
   2 tablespoons milk

Prepare and bake your favorite spice cake recipe or one-layer size spice cake mix. Pare, core, and slice pears. Combine sugar, water, and cinnamon candies; heat to boiling; add pear slices. Simmer over low heat till tender, 8 to 10 minutes; drain and cool. Arrange pear slices on slightly warm cake.

Combine butter or margarine, brown sugar, nuts, salt, and milk; spoon over pears. Place cake under broiler about 8 inches from heat; broil for 8 to 10 minutes, or till mixture bubbles and caramelizes slightly. Serve cake warm. Makes 9 servings.

BLUEBERRY BUCKLE

½ cup shortening
¾ cup sugar
1 well beaten egg
2 cups sifted all-purpose flour
2½ teaspoons baking powder
¼ teaspoon salt
½ cup milk
2 cups fresh blueberries
Cinnamon Crumbs

Cream shortening and sugar; add egg; beat till fluffy. Sift dry ingredients together; add alternately with milk. Spread in greased 11x7x1½-inch pan. Top with blueberries. Sprinkle Cinnamon Crumbs over berries. Bake at 350° about 45 minutes. Cut in squares. Serve warm with cream. Serves 8 to 10.

Cinnamon Crumbs: Mix ½ cup *each* sugar, sifted flour, and ½ teaspoon ground cinnamon. Cut in ¼ cup butter till crumbly.

PEAR-BERRY COFFEECAKE

3 fresh pears, pared and cored
1 teaspoon lemon juice
½ cup brown sugar
½ cup sifted all-purpose flour
¼ teaspoon ground nutmeg
¼ cup butter or margarine
1 13½-ounce package blueberry
    muffin mix

Slice pears lengthwise into eighths. Sprinkle with lemon. Mix next 3 ingredients; cut in butter. Prepare muffin mix using package directions. Turn into greased 9x9x2-inch pan. Top with pears. Spoon crumbly mixture over. Bake at 400° about 35 minutes. Serves 9.

APPLESAUCE DOUGHNUTS

Blend 1 tablespoon shortening with ¾ cup brown sugar; stir in ½ cup applesauce and 1 egg. Sift together 2 cups sifted all-purpose flour, ½ teaspoon soda, ¼ teaspoon *each* salt, ground nutmeg, and ground cinnamon. Gradually stir into applesauce mixture. Roll ½-inch thick on floured surface. Cut with doughnut cutter; fry in deep hot fat (365°) till browned on both sides, about 3 minutes. Drain; roll in cinnamon-sugar. Makes 12.

OATMEAL BANANA BREAD

2 cups packaged biscuit mix
1 cup quick-cooking rolled oats
½ cup chopped California walnuts
¼ cup butter or margarine
½ cup sugar
2 eggs
1 cup mashed ripe banana
¼ cup milk

Combine first 3 ingredients; set aside. Cream butter and sugar till light and fluffy. Beat in eggs, one at a time; stir in bananas and milk. Add dry ingredients, all at once, stirring just till moistened. Turn into greased 9x5x3-inch loaf pan. Bake at 350° about 40 minutes or till done. Remove from pan; cool.

MINCE-NUT BREAD

Sift together 2½ cups sifted all-purpose flour, ¾ cup sugar, ½ teaspoon soda, and ¼ teaspoon salt. Combine 1 cup prepared mincemeat, ½ cup water, ½ cup melted shortening, cooled, ¼ cup molasses, and 1 slightly beaten egg. Add to dry ingredients, mixing well. Stir in ½ cup chopped California walnuts. Turn into greased 9x5x3-inch pan. Bake at 350° about 1¼ hours. Cool; remove from pan. Wrap; refrigerate overnight.

APRICOT-NUT LOAF

1 cup sugar
¼ cup shortening
1 egg
¾ cup milk
1 teaspoon shredded orange peel
¾ cup orange juice
3 cups sifted all-purpose flour
3½ teaspoons baking powder
1 teaspoon salt
1 cup finely chopped dried apricots
½ cup chopped California walnuts

Cream sugar and shortening; beat in egg. Blend in milk, orange peel and juice. Sift together dry ingredients; add. Stir in apricots and nuts. Bake in greased 9x5x3-inch pan in a moderate oven (350°) 65 to 70 minutes. Cool; remove from pan. Wrap in foil and store overnight before serving.

DATE-NUT BREAD

2¾ cups sifted all-purpose flour
4 teaspoons baking powder
1 teaspoon salt
¾ cup brown sugar
1 beaten egg
1½ cups milk
3 tablespoons salad oil
1⅓ cups snipped pitted dates
¾ cup chopped California walnuts

Sift together the first 3 ingredients; stir in sugar. Combine egg, milk, and oil. Stir into dry ingredients; beat. Stir in the dates and nuts. Turn into greased 9x5x3-inch pan. Bake at 350° about 1 hour. Cool. Remove from pan.

CRANBERRY-BANANA BREAD

¼ cup butter or margarine
1 cup sugar
1 egg
2 cups sifted all-purpose flour
3 teaspoons baking powder
½ teaspoon salt
½ teaspoon ground cinnamon
1 cup mashed ripe banana
¼ cup milk
1 teaspoon shredded orange peel
1½ cups fresh cranberries, ground and drained
1 cup chopped pecans

Cream butter and sugar; add egg; beat. Sift dry ingredients together; add alternately with combined banana, milk, and orange peel. Stir in berries and nuts. Turn into greased 9x5x3-inch pan. Bake at 350° 60 to 65 minutes.

OATMEAL-RAISIN BREAD

Sift together 2 cups sifted all-purpose flour, 3 teaspoons baking powder, 1 teaspoon salt, 1 teaspoon ground cinnamon, and ¼ teaspoon ground nutmeg. Stir in ¾ cup *each* rolled oats and brown sugar. Combine 1 cup milk, 2 beaten eggs, and ¼ cup melted shortening, cooled; add to dry ingredients. Stir in ½ cup raisins; beat vigorously 30 seconds. Bake in greased 9x5x3-inch pan at 350° for 55 to 60 minutes. Cool slightly; remove from pan. Drizzle with confectioners' icing. Makes 1 loaf.

STRAWBERRY-NUT LOAF

Cream 1 cup butter, 1½ cups sugar, 1 teaspoon vanilla, and ¼ teaspoon lemon extract till light; add 4 eggs, one at a time, beating well after each. Sift together 3 cups sifted all-purpose flour, 1 teaspoon salt, ¾ teaspoon cream of tartar and ½ teaspoon soda.

Combine 1 cup strawberry jam and ½ cup dairy sour cream; add alternately with dry ingredients to creamed mixture. Stir in ½ cup broken walnuts. Pour into 2 paper-lined 8½x 4½x2½-inch loaf pans. Bake at 350° about 50 minutes. Cool 10 minutes. Remove.

APPLE-RAISIN LOAVES

1 package raisin-spice quick bread mix
1 cup apple juice
1 cup chopped pared apple
Apple Glaze

Prepare mix according to package directions, substituting apple juice for the liquid; stir in the chopped apple. Turn into 4 greased and lightly floured 4½x2¾x2¼-inch loaf pans. Bake at 350° for 35 minutes. While still warm, drizzle with *Apple Glaze:* Add enough apple juice to 1 cup confectioners' sugar to make of pourable consistency. Makes 4 loaves.

PRUNE-NUT BREAD

1 cup dried prunes
2 teaspoons shredded orange peel
1 cup orange juice
2 cups instant-type flour
¾ cup sugar
3 teaspoons baking powder
½ teaspoon salt
½ teaspoon ground cinnamon
2 eggs
2 tablespoons salad oil
½ cup chopped California walnuts

Snip prunes into greased 9x5x3-inch pan; add orange peel and juice; let stand ½ hour. Add remaining ingredients; beat well with fork till blended, about 2 minutes. Scrape pan after beating 1 minute. Bake at 350° for 50 to 55 minutes. Remove from pan; cool. Wrap in foil; store overnight for best slicing.

BLUEBERRY MUFFINS

1¾ cups sifted all-purpose flour
¼ cup sugar
2½ teaspoons baking powder
¾ teaspoon salt
1 well beaten egg
¾ cup milk
⅓ cup melted shortening
1 cup fresh blueberries *or* frozen blueberries thawed and drained

Sift together first 4 ingredients. Combine egg, milk, and shortening. Make well in center of dry ingredients; add egg mixture all at once. Stir quickly just till dry ingredients are moistened. Gently stir in blueberries. Fill greased muffin pans ⅔ full. Bake at 400° about 25 minutes or till golden brown. Makes 12.

APPLESAUCE PUFFS

Combine 2 cups packaged biscuit mix, ¼ cup sugar, and 1 teaspoon ground cinnamon. Add ½ cup applesauce, ¼ cup milk, 1 slightly beaten egg, and 2 tablespoons salad oil. *Beat vigorously* 30 seconds. Fill greased 2-inch muffin pans ⅔ full. Bake in hot oven (400°) 12 minutes or till done. Cool slightly; remove. Brush tops with 2 tablespoons melted butter or margarine; dip in ¼ cup sugar mixed with ¼ teaspoon ground cinnamon. Makes 24.

ORANGE-MINCE MUFFINS

1 beaten egg
½ cup prepared mincemeat
½ cup apple juice
1 14-ounce package orange muffin mix
1 cup sifted confectioners' sugar
4 teaspoons milk
¼ teaspoon rum extract

Combine the egg, mincemeat, and apple juice in mixing bowl. Add the muffin mix all at once; stir just till blended. Fill greased muffin pans half full. Bake in hot oven (400°) for about 15 minutes or till golden brown. Remove from pans immediately. Blend the confectioners' sugar with the milk and rum extract; drizzle over warm muffins. Serve warm. Makes 1 dozen muffins.

HOT CROSS MUFFINS

Mix together 2 cups packaged biscuit mix, ¼ cup sugar, ¼ teaspoon salt, 1 teaspoon ground cinnamon, 2 slightly beaten eggs, ¾ cup milk, 2 tablespoons salad oil, and 2 teaspoons shredded orange peel; beat vigorously 30 seconds. Add ½ cup currants. Fill greased muffin pans ⅔ full. Bake at 400° for 15 to 18 minutes. Cool slightly. Pipe on crosses of confectioners' icing. Serve warm. Makes 12.

DATE BRAN MUFFINS

2 tablespoons shortening
3 tablespoons sugar
1 egg
¾ cup milk
1 cup whole bran
¾ cup finely snipped dates
1 cup sifted all-purpose flour
2 teaspoons baking powder
½ teaspoon salt

Cream shortening and sugar; add egg and beat well. Stir in milk, bran, and dates. Sift dry ingredients together; add to date mixture, stirring just till moistened. Fill greased muffin pans ⅔ full. Bake in hot oven (425°) 20 to 25 minutes. Makes 1 dozen.

If desired, substitute raisins for dates.

SPICY FRUIT PUFFS

2 cups sifted all-purpose flour
3 teaspoons baking powder
1 teaspoon salt
½ teaspoon ground cinnamon
¼ teaspoon ground nutmeg
1 cup shredded pared apple
⅔ cup brown sugar
¼ cup chopped California walnuts
2 beaten eggs
⅔ cup milk
¼ cup shortening, melted and cooled
1 cup whole wheat *or* bran flakes

Sift together first 5 ingredients. Stir in apple, brown sugar, and walnuts. Combine eggs, milk, and shortening; add all at once, stirring just to blend. Fold in cereal flakes. Fill greased muffin pans ⅔ full. Bake at 400° for 15 to 20 minutes. Makes 12 muffins.

Tasty pancakes, waffles

BLUEBERRY SYRUP

  1 1-pound can (2 cups) blueberries
  ½ cup light corn syrup
  Dash salt

With electric blender or mixer, blend blueberries till smooth. In saucepan, combine the blended berries, corn syrup, and salt. Bring to boiling; boil gently, stirring constantly, for 5 to 7 minutes, or till consistency of syrup. Serve warm. Makes 2 cups.

SPICY PINEAPPLE SYRUP

  ½ 10-ounce jar pineapple ice cream topping
  ¼ cup light corn syrup
  1½ teaspoons lemon juice
  Dash cinnamon
  Dash nutmeg

In saucepan, combine ice cream topping, syrup, lemon juice, cinnamon, and nutmeg. Heat and stir. Serve warm. Makes ¾ cup.

STRAWBERRY SYRUP

  1 10-ounce package frozen sliced strawberries, thawed
  ½ cup light corn syrup
  Dash salt

With electric blender or mixer, blend strawberries till smooth. In saucepan, combine blended strawberries, syrup, and salt. Bring to boiling; boil gently, stirring constantly, 5 minutes. Serve warm. Makes 1½ cups.

HONEY-BANANA SYRUP

In a saucepan, combine ½ cup honey, ¼ cup orange juice, 1 tablespoon lemon juice, and dash salt. On cutting board, mash 1 ripe banana with a fork. (Medium banana will yield about ½ cup.) Stir mashed banana into honey mixture. Heat and stir syrup gently. Serve warm. Makes 1¼ cups.

FRESH APPLE WAFFLES

  1¾ cups sifted all-purpose flour
  2½ teaspoons baking powder
  ½ teaspoon salt
  1 tablespoon sugar
  2 beaten egg yolks
  1¼ cups milk
  2 tablespoons salad oil
  2 apples, pared, cored, and finely chopped
  2 stiffly beaten egg whites
  1 cup brown sugar
  1 cup apple cider
  1 tablespoon butter or margarine
  ½ teaspoon lemon juice
  ¼ teaspoon ground cinnamon
  ⅛ teaspoon ground nutmeg

Sift together first 4 ingredients. Combine egg yolks, milk, and salad oil. Add to dry ingredients; mix well. Stir in apples. Fold in egg whites. Bake in hot waffle baker. Makes 4 cups of batter or about 12 waffles.

Serve with *Hot Cider Sauce:* In saucepan, combine sugar, cider, butter, lemon juice, cinnamon, and nutmeg. Bring to boiling; simmer 15 minutes or till slightly thickened.

ORANGE COCONUT WAFFLES

  2¼ cups sifted all-purpose flour
  4 teaspoons baking powder
  ¾ teaspoon salt
  1½ tablespoons sugar
      • • •
  2 beaten eggs
  2¼ cups milk
  ½ cup salad oil
  2 tablespoons flaked coconut
  1 tablespoon shredded orange peel

Sift together dry ingredients. Combine eggs, milk, and salad oil. Just before baking, add milk mixture to dry ingredients, beating just till moistened (batter will be thin).

Combine flaked coconut and orange peel. Pour batter onto preheated waffle baker; quickly top each waffle with some coconut-peel mixture; bake. Makes 10 to 12 waffles.

Great pair Blueberry Pancakes and **Whipped Orange Butter:** Whip ½ cup soft butter with grated peel and juice from ½ small orange.

BLUEBERRY PANCAKES

  1 cup fresh, frozen, or canned
     blueberries
  1 well beaten egg
  1 cup milk
  ¼ cup butter or margarine, melted
  1 cup sifted all-purpose flour
2½ teaspoons baking powder
  2 tablespoons sugar
  ¾ teaspoon salt

Drain frozen or canned blueberries thoroughly. Combine egg, milk, and butter. Sift together dry ingredients; gradually add to egg mixture, beating with electric or rotary beater. Use ¼ cup measure to drop batter on hot, lightly greased griddle. Sprinkle about 2 tablespoons berries over each cake. When underside is golden, turn and brown other side. Serve with Orange Butter. Makes 8.

APPLESAUCE PANCAKES

  2 cups packaged biscuit mix
  2 eggs
  1 cup milk
  1 1-pound can (2 cups) applesauce
  1 10-ounce jar (1 cup) apple jelly
  ½ teaspoon ground cinnamon
     Dash ground cloves
     Dash salt

In medium bowl, combine biscuit mix, eggs, milk, and *1 cup* of the applesauce; beat till smooth. Bake on hot, lightly greased griddle, using about ⅓ cup batter for each pancake. Makes about one dozen large pancakes.

Serve hot with *Spiced Apple Syrup:* In small saucepan, combine the remaining 1 cup applesauce, the apple jelly, cinnamon, cloves, and salt. Cook and stir till jelly melts and syrup is hot. Makes 2 cups syrup.

Sandwiches starring fruit

PEACHY HAM SWISSER

1 loaf French bread
Leaf lettuce
6 slices boiled ham
4 slices process Swiss cheese,
halved diagonally
1 1-pound can peach halves, well
drained
½ cup mayonnaise or salad dressing
2 tablespoons chili sauce
1 tablespoon pickle relish

Cut French bread in half lengthwise; wrap top half and store. To steady loaf, cut thin slice of crust from bottom of loaf; spread top of bread with butter. Arrange lettuce and ham on bread; top with cheese and peaches. Combine mayonnaise, chili sauce, and relish; drizzle over sandwich. Makes 5 or 6 servings.

FRUIT TEA SANDWICHES

1 3-ounce package cream cheese,
softened
2 tablespoons drained crushed
pineapple
½ teaspoon grated lemon peel
Dash salt
½ cup halved seedless green grapes
¼ cup miniature marshmallows
Raisin or nut bread, buttered

Combine cream cheese, pineapple, lemon peel, and salt; beat till fluffy. Add grapes and marshmallows. Spread between slices of buttered raisin or nut bread. Makes 1 cup.

PEANUT-BANANA SPREAD

1 3-ounce package cream cheese,
softened
¼ cup peanut butter
1 tablespoon honey
1 medium banana, mashed
Raisin bread

Blend first 4 ingredients; spread between slices of buttered raisin bread. Makes 1 cup.

AVOCADO BACON SANDWICH

¼ cup buttermilk
½ cup mayonnaise or salad dressing
2 tablespoons chopped onion
½ teaspoon Worcestershire sauce
Dash garlic salt
2 ounces blue cheese, crumbled
(½ cup)
• • •
6 slices rye bread, toasted
Leaf lettuce
12 slices bacon, crisp-cooked and
drained
3 medium avocados, seeded, peeled,
and sliced
1 lemon, cut in 6 wedges

Put buttermilk, mayonnaise, onion, Worcestershire, and garlic salt into blender container; add *half* of the cheese; cover and run on high speed till smooth. Stir in remaining cheese. Spread each piece of toast generously with the blue cheese dressing. Top each with lettuce, 2 slices bacon, and avocado slices. Drizzle with additional dressing; garnish with lemon wedges. Makes 6 servings.

APPLE TURKEY SANDWICHES

4 slices buttered toast
4 large slices cooked turkey
Salt and pepper
• • •
½ cup mayonnaise or salad dressing
⅓ cup finely chopped celery
¼ cup snipped green onions and tops
½ cup coarsely shredded cored,
pared tart apple
½ to 1 teaspoon curry powder
¼ teaspoon salt
Dash pepper

Arrange toast on baking sheet. Cover with turkey; sprinkle with salt and pepper. Mix together mayonnaise, celery, onion, apple, curry powder, salt, and pepper; spread over turkey. Broil 7 to 8 inches from the heat 5 to 8 minutes or till heated through and lightly browned. Makes 4 servings.

Hong Kong Hamburger sports a tangy sweet-sour pineapple glaze. Oriental Tuna Sandwich is spiked with curry and mellowed by avocado.

HONG KONG HAMBURGER

Combine 1 pound ground beef, 1 beaten egg, ½ teaspoon salt, and dash pepper. Cut 1 loaf French bread in half lengthwise. Wrap top half and store. Spread meat mixture over bottom half, bringing mixture right to edges. Broil till brown, 8 to 10 minutes.

Meanwhile, make glaze. Drain ¼ cup syrup from one 1-pound 4½-ounce can sliced pineapple. Blend ⅓ cup brown sugar and 2 teaspoons cornstarch; stir in reserved syrup, 3 tablespoons red wine vinegar, 1 tablespoon soy sauce, and 1 tablespoon Worcestershire sauce. Cook and stir to boiling.

Remove loaf from broiler; brush with some of the glaze. Top meat with pineapple half-slices and green pepper rings. Brush with remaining glaze; return to broiler for 2 minutes or till topping is heated. Garnish with red peppers. Makes 4 to 6 servings.

ORIENTAL TUNA SANDWICH

½ cup mayonnaise or salad dressing
2 tablespoons minced onion
2 teaspoons lemon juice
2 teaspoons soy sauce
1 teaspoon curry powder
2 6½- or 7-ounce cans tuna, drained
1 5-ounce can water chestnuts, drained and sliced
1 loaf French bread
Butter or margarine, softened
Lettuce
4 cherry tomatoes, halved
1 avocado, peeled and sliced

Blend first 5 ingredients. Add tuna and water chestnuts; toss lightly. Cut bread in half lengthwise; wrap top half and store. Spread bottom half with butter. Top with lettuce, tuna, tomatoes, and avocado. Serves 6.

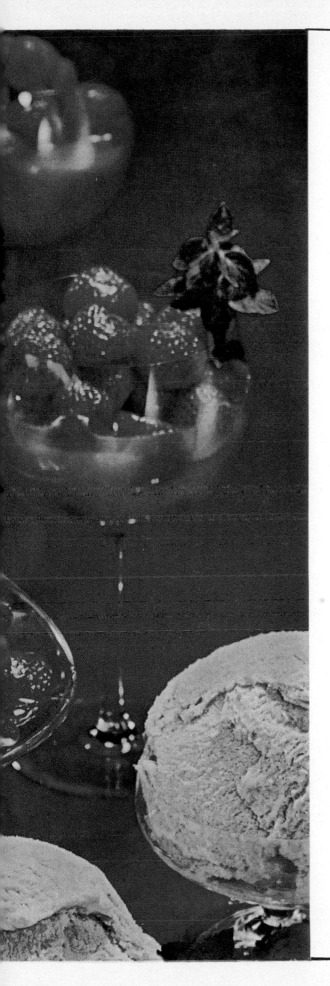

DESSERTS AND REFRESHERS

Strawberry-rhubarb Shortcake, Berry Cup, and Rhubarb Ice Cream—three of the desserts to come. Pies, cakes, warm and chilly desserts, sodas and sundaes, too!

Fabulous fruit pies

PLAIN PASTRY

For one single-crust pie or 4 to 6 tart shells:

- 1½ cups sifted all-purpose flour
- ½ teaspoon salt
- ½ cup shortening
- 4 to 5 tablespoons cold water

For one 8-, 9-, or 10-inch double-crust or lattice-top pie, two 8-, 9-, or 10-inch single-crust pies, or 6 to 8 tart shells:

- 2 cups sifted all-purpose flour
- 1 teaspoon salt
- ⅔ cup shortening
- 5 to 7 tablespoons cold water

Sift together flour and salt; cut in shortening with pastry blender or blending fork till pieces are the size of small peas. (For extra tender pastry, cut in *half* the shortening till mixture looks like cornmeal. Then cut in remaining till like small peas.) Sprinkle 1 tablespoon water over part of mixture. Gently toss with fork; push to side of bowl. Sprinkle next table-spoon water over dry part; toss lightly; push to moistened part at side. Repeat till all is moistened. Form into ball. (For double-crust and lattice-top pies, divide dough for lower and upper crust. Form each portion into ball.) Flatten ball on lightly floured surface. Roll from center to edge till dough is ⅛ inch thick.

To bake single-crust pie shells: Fit pastry into pie plate, trim ½ to 1 inch beyond edge; fold under and flute. Prick bottom and sides well with fork. Bake in a very hot oven (450°) for 10 to 12 minutes or till golden.

For lattice-top pie: Trim lower crust ½ inch beyond edge of pie plate. Roll remaining dough ⅛ inch thick. Cut strips of pastry ½ to ¾ inch wide with pastry wheel or knife. Lay strips on filled pie at 1-inch intervals. Fold back alternate strips as you weave cross-strips. Trim lattice even with outer rim; fold lower crust over strips. Seal and flute.

For double-crust pie: Trim lower crust even with rim of pie plate. Cut slits in upper crust. Fit loosely over filling; trim ½ inch beyond edge; tuck under edge of lower crust. Flute.

APPLE CRUMB PIE

- ¼ cup shortening
- 1 cup grated sharp process American cheese
- 1 cup sifted all-purpose flour
- ½ teaspoon salt
- 2 tablespoons cold water
- 5 cups apples, pared, cored, and sliced
- ¼ cup sugar
- ½ teaspoon ground cinnamon
- 1 cup sifted all-purpose flour
- ⅓ cup brown sugar
- ¼ cup butter or margarine, softened
- ⅓ cup grated sharp process American cheese

To prepare crust, cream together first 2 in-gredients. Sift together the 1 cup flour and salt; add to cheese mixture. Gradually add the water. Mix. Roll on lightly floured sur-face. Line 9-inch pie plate; flute edge.

Combine apples, sugar, and cinnamon; arrange in pastry-lined pie plate. For topping, combine remaining ingredients and crumble over apples. Bake at 375° for 35 minutes. If crust browns too rapidly, cover rim with foil.

For apple trim, combine 1 cup sugar, 1 cup water, and dash salt; simmer 5 minutes. Cook six ½-inch apple slices in syrup till tender. Cool; drain; arrange on pie.

PEACH-MINCE PIE

- Pastry for 2-crust 9-inch pie
- 2½ cups prepared mincemeat
- 1 1-pound can (2 cups) sliced peaches, drained

Line 9-inch pie plate with pastry. Fill with a mixture of the mincemeat and peaches. Ad-just top crust, cutting slits for escape of steam; seal. Brush crust with milk and sprinkle with sugar. Bake in hot oven (400°) 45 minutes or till crust is browned.

Cheese pastry and topping gives Apple → Crumb Pie a twist. Canned peaches and mincemeat make Peach-mince Pie easy.

APPLE-RAISIN PIE

　　Pastry for 2-crust 9-inch pie
¾ cup sugar
2 tablespoons all-purpose flour
¼ teaspoon salt
½ cup water
1 cup raisins

• • •

3 to 4 tart apples*
2 tablespoons rum
　　Sliced sharp process American cheese

Prepare pastry. Blend sugar, flour, and salt; stir in water and raisins. Cook, stirring constantly, till mixture thickens, about 5 minutes. Pare apples and slice thin; add to raisin mixture along with rum. Line 9-inch pie plate with pastry; fill with apple-raisin mixture. Cut design in top crust. Adjust top crust; crimp edge. Sprinkle top with sugar for sparkle. Gently fold a strip of foil or pie tape around rim of crust covering fluted edge. (This guards against boil-over in oven and overbrowning.) Bake in a hot oven (400°) 40 to 50 minutes or till done. Before serving, top pie with 6 triangles of cheese; broil to melt cheese. Serve warm.

　　*If apples lack tartness, sprinkle slices with 1 tablespoon lemon juice. *Or* use one 1-pound 4-ounce can (2½ cups) sliced pie apples. Drain apples, *reserving liquid*. Use apple liquid in place of water for plumping the raisins.

GOOSEBERRY PIE

　　Pastry for 2-crust 9-inch pie
3 cups gooseberries (about 1 pound)
1½ cups sugar
3 tablespoons quick-cooking tapioca
¼ teaspoon salt
2 tablespoons butter or margarine

Prepare pastry. Stem and rinse berries. Crush ½ *cup* berries; combine sugar, tapioca, and salt and mix with crushed berries. Cook and stir till mixture boils; cook 2 minutes. Remove from heat. Add remaining whole berries. Pour into pastry lined 9-inch pie plate; dot with butter. Adjust top crust cutting slits for escape of steam; seal. Brush top with milk and sprinkle with sugar. Bake at 400° about 35 minutes or till done.

CHERRY RHUBARB PIE

Winning combination—rosy rhubarb and cherries—

　　Pastry for 9-inch lattice-top pie
1 pound rhubarb, cut in ½-inch slices (about 4 cups)
1 1-pound can (2 cups) pitted tart red cherries (water pack), drained
1¼ cups sugar
¼ cup quick-cooking tapioca
5 drops red food coloring

Prepare pastry. Combine remaining ingredients; let stand 15 minutes. Line 9-inch pie plate with pastry; pour in filling. Adjust lattice top; seal; flute edge. Bake in hot oven (400°) 40 to 50 minutes. Serve warm.

BLUEBERRY PIE

Like spice? Add ½ teaspoon of ground cinnamon and dash ground nutmeg to filling—

　　Pastry for 2-crust 9-inch pie
4 cups fresh blueberries
¾ to 1 cup sugar
3 tablespoons all-purpose flour
½ teaspoon grated lemon peel
　　Dash salt
1 to 2 teaspoons lemon juice
1 tablespoon butter or margarine

Prepare pastry. Combine berries, sugar, flour, lemon peel, and salt. Line 9-inch pie plate with pastry; pour in filling. Drizzle with lemon juice and dot with butter. Adjust top crust cutting slits for escape of steam; seal. Bake in hot oven (400°) 35 to 40 minutes. If desired, sprinkle top with confectioners' sugar and few fresh berries. Serve warm.

FRESH PEACH CUSTARD PIE

　　Place 3 cups sliced fresh peaches in an *unbaked* 9-inch pastry shell. Combine ⅔ cup sugar, ¼ teaspoon salt, and 2 tablespoons all-purpose flour with 2 beaten eggs; stir in 1 cup scalded light cream. Pour over peaches. Sprinkle with ½ teaspoon ground nutmeg. Bake in moderate oven (375°) 30 to 40 minutes or till knife inserted halfway between center and edge comes out clean.

Cranberry-pear Pie, made from fresh pears and canned whole cranberry sauce, gets its sparkly look from a sprinkling of sugar.

SLICED PEAR PIE

Fresh pears with the tang of lemon—

    Pastry for 9-inch lattice-top pie
5 fresh pears, pared and sliced
¾ to 1 cup sugar
¼ cup all-purpose flour
½ teaspoon ground cinnamon
    Dash salt
½ teaspoon shredded lemon peel
2 tablespoons lemon juice
2 tablespoons butter or margarine

Prepare pastry. Toss together the pears, sugar, flour, cinnamon, salt, lemon peel and juice. Arrange in pastry-lined 9-inch pie plate. Dot with butter or margarine. Adjust lattice top; seal and flute edge. Cover edge of pie with foil. Bake at 425° about 35 minutes, removing foil after 25 minutes.

CRANBERRY-PEAR PIE

    Pastry for 9-inch lattice-top pie
½ cup sugar
3 tablespoons all-purpose flour
¼ teaspoon ground cinnamon
    Dash salt
1 tablespoon lemon juice
1 cup whole cranberry sauce
3 cups sliced fresh pears
1 tablespoon butter or margarine

Prepare pastry. Combine sugar, flour, cinnamon, and salt. Blend with lemon juice and cranberry sauce. Lightly stir in pear slices. Turn into pastry-lined pie plate. Dot with butter. Adjust lattice top; seal; flute edge. Sprinkle top lightly with sugar. To prevent overbrowning, cover edge of pastry with foil strip. Remove foil a few minutes before pie is done. Bake at 400° for 35 to 40 minutes.

CONCORD GRAPE PIE

Slip skins from 1½ pounds (about 4 cups) ripe Concord grapes; set skins aside. Bring pulp to boiling; reduce heat and simmer, uncovered, 5 minutes. Press through sieve to remove seeds. Add skins to pulp.

Combine 1 cup sugar, ⅓ cup all-purpose flour, and ¼ teaspoon salt. Add 1 tablespoon lemon juice, 2 tablespoons butter or margarine, melted, and grape mixture. Pour into *unbaked* 9-inch pastry shell. Bake in hot oven (400°) 25 minutes. Meanwhile prepare topping: Sift together ½ cup all-purpose flour and ½ cup sugar. Cut in ¼ cup butter or margarine till crumbly. Remove pie from oven; sprinkle mixture over top and bake 15 minutes longer. Arrange pastry leaves atop.

Pastry grape leaves: Cut leaf design from pastry with a sharp knife. Mark leaf veins with top of knife. Bake on cookie sheet at 450° about 8 to 10 minutes. Arrange on hot pie.

SOUR CREAM PLUM PIE

    6 tablespoons butter or margarine
    ½ cup sugar
    1 cup sifted all-purpose flour
    ½ teaspoon salt
    ½ teaspoon ground cinnamon
    ¼ teaspoon baking powder
    1 1-pound can purple plums, drained
    1 slightly beaten egg
    1 cup dairy sour cream
    2 tablespoons sugar
    1 teaspoon vanilla
    ¼ cup chopped California walnuts

Cream first 2 ingredients. Sift dry ingredients together. Blend into creamed mixture till crumbly. Press in 9-inch pie plate. Bake at 350° for 20 minutes. Pit and halve plums; arrange skin side down over crust. Mix remaining ingredients. Spread over plums. Bake 5 to 6 minutes or till set. Serve warm.

Best "grapevine news" ever! Old-fashioned Concord Grape Pie has a crumbly baked-on topper. Pastry grape leaves garnish top.

PEACH MARSHMALLOW PIE

Drain one 1-pound 13-ounce can (3½ cups) sliced peaches, reserving 1¼ cups syrup. Reserve 6 peach slices; cut up remainder. Combine ¼ cup sugar, 1 envelope unflavored gelatin, and ¼ teaspoon salt. Blend in reserved syrup; add 1 cup miniature marshmallows. Cook and stir till marshmallows melt. Blend some of hot mixture into 1 beaten egg; return to hot mixture. Cook and stir 2 to 3 minutes. Add 1 teaspoon shredded lemon peel and 4 teaspoons lemon juice. Cover; cool till mixture begins to set. Fold in cut up peaches and ½ cup whipping cream, whipped; spoon into *baked* 9-inch pastry shell. Chill 3 to 4 hours. Top with whipped cream and reserved peach slices.

STRAWBERRY-MALLOW PIE

3½ cups miniature marshmallows
¾ cup milk
1 cup whipping cream, whipped
½ teaspoon vanilla
1 *baked* 9-inch pastry shell
1 1 pound 5 ounce can strawberry pie filling

Set aside ½ cup marshmallows; melt remaining marshmallows with milk over low heat, stirring constantly. Chill, without stirring, till partially set. Fold in whipped cream, vanilla, and dash salt. Spoon *half* the mixture into pastry shell. Cover with pie filling, reserving ½ cup. Fold reserved marshmallows into remaining marshmallow-cream mixture; spread over strawberry layer. Garnish with reserved filling. Chill 6 hours or overnight.

CRANBERRY CHEESE PIE

Toast 1⅓ cups flaked coconut in a moderate oven (350°) about 10 minutes, stirring often. Combine with ¼ cup melted butter or margarine. Press into an 8-inch pie plate.

Beat one 8-ounce package cream cheese till softened. Whip ½ cup whipping cream till thickened, but not stiff. Add ¼ cup sugar and ½ teaspoon vanilla. Gradually add to cream cheese, beating till smooth and creamy. Fold in one 1-pound can whole cranberry sauce. Spoon into coconut crust. Chill till firm.

BANANA APRICOT PIE

2 cups snipped dried apricots
1½ cups water
1¼ cups sugar
3 tablespoons all-purpose flour
3 beaten egg yolks
2 tablespoons butter or margarine
2 medium bananas, sliced (2 cups)
1 *baked* 9-inch pastry shell
Meringue

Combine apricots and water. Cover; simmer 10 minutes or till tender. Combine sugar, flour, and ¼ teaspoon salt; stir into apricot mixture. Heat to boiling; boil 2 minutes; stir constantly. Blend some of hot mixture into egg yolks; return to hot mixture. Cook and stir to boiling. Add butter. Place bananas in pastry shell; top with filling.

Prepare *Meringue:* Beat 3 egg whites with ½ teaspoon vanilla and ¼ teaspoon cream of tartar to soft peaks. Gradually add 6 tablespoons sugar, beating to stiff peaks. Spread meringue over filling, sealing to edge of pastry. Bake at 350° for 12 to 15 minutes.

LEMON SOUR CREAM PIE

1 cup sugar
3 tablespoons cornstarch
1 cup milk
3 slightly beaten egg yolks
¼ cup butter or margarine
1 teaspoon shredded lemon peel
¼ cup lemon juice
1 cup dairy sour cream
1 *baked* 9-inch pastry shell
Meringue

Combine sugar, cornstarch, and dash salt. Slowly add the milk, stirring constantly. Cook and stir till mixture thickens and boils. Blend small amount of hot mixture into beaten egg yolks; return to hot mixture. Cook and stir 2 minutes. Add butter or margarine, lemon peel and juice. Cover; cool. Fold in sour cream. Spoon into pastry shell.

Prepare *Meringue:* Beat 3 egg whites with ½ teaspoon vanilla and ¼ teaspoon cream of tartar to soft peaks. Gradually add 6 tablespoons sugar, beating to stiff peaks. Spread meringue over filling, sealing to edge of pastry. Bake at 350° for 12 to 15 minutes.

TANGELO CHIFFON PIE

1 envelope (1 tablespoon) unflavored gelatin
½ cup sugar
Dash salt
4 egg yolks
½ cup lemon juice
¾ cup tangelo *or* tangerine juice

• • •

½ teaspoon grated lemon peel
½ teaspoon grated tangelo or tangerine peel
4 egg whites
⅓ cup sugar
1 *baked* 9-inch pastry shell

In a saucepan, mix gelatin, ½ cup sugar, and salt. Beat together egg yolks and fruit juices; stir into gelatin mixture. Cook and stir over medium heat till mixture comes to boiling. Remove from heat; mix in peels. Chill, stirring occasionally, till partially set. Beat egg whites till soft peaks form. Gradually add ⅓ cup sugar; beat to stiff peaks. Fold in gelatin mixture. Pile into pastry shell; chill till firm. Garnish with whipped cream and tangelo *or tangerine sections.*

COCKTAIL CHIFFON PIE

In top of double boiler, soften 1 envelope (1 tablespoon) unflavored gelatin in ½ cup cold water. Add 3 slightly beaten egg yolks and dash salt. Cook and stir over hot, *not boiling,* water till gelatin dissolves and mixture thickens, about 7 minutes. Remove from heat; stir in one 6-ounce can frozen lemonade concentrate (not thawed). Chill, stirring occasionally, till partially set.

Beat 3 egg whites till soft peaks form. Gradually add ½ cup sugar, beating to stiff peaks. Fold in gelatin mixture. Drain one 1-pound can (2 cups) fruit cocktail. Reserving ½ cup fruit, fold remaining fruit into gelatin mixture. If necessary, chill till mixture mounds slightly when spooned. Pile into a *baked* 9-inch pastry shell. Chill till firm. Before serving, arrange reserved fruit in a ring atop pie. Trim with mint leaves.

← Minneola Tangelos inspired this Tangelo Chiffon Pie. Tangerine Peel Chrysanthemum is meant to be eaten and admired.

DATE CHIFFON PIE

Cheese pastry
1 envelope (1 tablespoon) unflavored gelatin
¼ cup sugar
2 egg yolks
½ cup orange juice
⅓ cup lemon juice
½ cup light cream
2 egg whites
¼ cup sugar
1½ cups snipped dates

Prepare *Cheese Pastry:* Sift together 1 cup sifted all-purpose flour and ½ teaspoon salt. Cut in ⅓ cup shortening. Add ½ cup shredded sharp process American cheese; toss lightly. Gradually sprinkle 3 tablespoons cold water over mixture, tossing with fork till moistened. Roll out on floured surface to ⅛ inch. Fit into 8-inch pie plate; crimp edges. Prick crust. Bake at 450° for 8 to 10 minutes.

In a saucepan, mix the gelatin and ¼ cup sugar. Beat together the egg yolks and fruit juices; stir into gelatin mixture. Cook and stir over medium heat just till mixture comes to boiling and is slightly thickened. Cool; stir in cream; chill till slightly thickened. Beat egg whites with dash salt till soft peaks form. Add ¼ cup sugar gradually; beat till stiff peaks form. Fold in gelatin mixture, then dates. Turn into cooled pastry. Chill firm.

STRAWBERRY TARTS

1 cup sugar
2 tablespoons cornstarch
1 quart fresh strawberries
1 tablespoon butter or margarine
1 3-ounce package strawberry-flavored gelatin
1 tablespoon lemon juice
6 to 8 *baked* tart shells, cooled

In saucepan, combine sugar and cornstarch. Mash *1 cup* of the berries; add water to make 2 cups. Stir into sugar mixture. Cook and stir till boiling; boil 2 minutes. Remove from heat. Add butter, gelatin, and lemon juice; stir till gelatin dissolves. Chill till partially set. Spoon ⅓ of the gelatin mixture into tart shells; top with the whole berries. Spoon remaining gelatin over berries; chill.

MANDARIN ANGEL PIE

Prepare Meringue Shell following directions given in the recipe Strawberry Angel Pie. Combine in a saucepan one 3⅝-ounce package lemon pudding and pie filling mix (dry), ½ cup sugar, and ¼ cup water. Blend in 3 egg yolks. Drain one 11-ounce can mandarin oranges, reserving syrup. To reserved syrup add 1 tablespoon lemon juice plus enough water to equal 1¾ cups. Stir into pudding mixture; cook and stir till mixture comes to a full boil over medium heat. Remove from heat; cool completely. Fold in ½ cup whipping cream, whipped, and ¾ *cup* of the oranges. Spoon into prepared Meringue Shell. Chill overnight. Top with whipped cream and remaining orange segments.

FROZEN MINCEMEAT TARTS

1 quart vanilla ice cream
1 cup prepared mincemeat
1 teaspoon grated orange peel
8 *baked* tart shells

Stir ice cream to soften; fold in mincemeat and peel. Fill shells; freeze. Before serving, top with whipped cream and toasted almonds.

LEMON ICE CREAM PIE

6 tablespoons butter or margarine
⅓ cup lemon juice
1 cup sugar
2 eggs
2 egg yolks
1 pint vanilla ice cream, softened
1 *baked* 9-inch pastry shell
2 egg whites
¼ cup sugar
1 teaspoon grated lemon peel

In saucepan, combine first 3 ingredients and dash salt. Beat eggs and egg yolks slightly; stir into lemon mixture. Cook and stir over low heat till mixture boils; chill. Spread ice cream in pastry shell; top with lemon mixture; freeze. Beat egg whites with dash salt till soft peaks form; gradually add sugar; beat till stiff peaks form. Fold in peel. Spread over frozen pie; seal. Bake at 500° about 3 minutes or till golden. Serve at once.

STRAWBERRY ANGEL PIE

3 egg whites
1 teaspoon vanilla
¼ teaspoon cream of tartar
1 cup sugar
1 3-ounce package strawberry-flavored gelatin
1¼ cups boiling water
1 cup sliced fresh strawberries *or* 1 10-ounce package frozen sliced strawberries, thawed and drained
1 cup whipping cream, whipped

Prepare **Meringue Shell:** Have egg whites at room temperature. Add vanilla, cream of tartar, and dash salt. Beat till frothy. Gradually add sugar, a little at a time, beating till very stiff peaks form and sugar is dissolved. Spoon into lightly greased 9-inch pie plate and shape into shell, swirling sides high. Bake at 275° for 1 hour. Turn off heat and let dry in oven (door closed) at least 2 hours.

Dissolve gelatin in boiling water. Chill until consistency of unbeaten egg white. Fold in strawberries and whipped cream. Chill until mixture mounds slightly when spooned. Pile into meringue shell. Chill 4 to 6 hours or overnight. Garnish with additional whipped cream and strawberry halves.

BLUEBERRY STRATA PIE

Drain, reserving syrups, one 1-pound can blueberries and one 8¾-ounce can crushed pineapple. Blend one 8-ounce package cream cheese, softened, with 3 tablespoons sugar, 1 tablespoon milk, and ½ teaspoon vanilla. Set aside 2 tablespoons pineapple; stir remaining into cheese mixture. Spread on bottom of *baked* 9-inch pastry shell; chill.

Blend ¼ cup sugar, 2 tablespoons cornstarch, and ¼ teaspoon salt. Combine reserved syrups; measure 1½ cups; blend into cornstarch mixture. Cook and stir till thickened. Stir in blueberries and 1 teaspoon lemon juice; cool. Pour over cheese layer; chill. Top with ½ cup whipping cream, whipped, and reserved pineapple.

Bake the meringue shell for Strawberry → Angel Pie early in the day, then whip up the easy strawberry filling and chill.

Fruit-dazzled shortcakes

BASIC SHORTCAKES

For 8-inch biscuit:

Mix well with fork 2 cups packaged biscuit mix, 2 tablespoons sugar, 1 beaten egg, 1/4 cup melted butter or margarine, and 2/3 cup light cream; beat vigorously 30 seconds. Spread dough in greased 8x1 1/2-inch round pan, building up edges slightly. Bake at 450° for 15 to 18 minutes or till done. Remove from pan; cool on rack 5 minutes.

Place on serving plate. With serrated knife, split in 2 layers; lift top off carefully. Spread bottom layer with softened butter. Spoon fruit mixture between layers and atop. Cut in wedges and serve warm.

For 6 individual biscuits:

Sift together 2 cups sifted all-purpose flour, 1 tablespoon sugar, 3 teaspoons baking powder, and 1/2 teaspoon salt. Cut in 6 tablespoons butter or margarine till mixture resembles coarse crumbs. Combine 1 beaten egg and 2/3 cup milk; add all at once to dry ingredients, stirring only to moisten. Turn dough out on floured surface; knead gently about 30 seconds. Pat or roll to 1/2-inch thickness. With floured 2 1/2-inch cutter, cut out 6 biscuits. Bake on ungreased baking sheet at 450° about 10 minutes. Split shortcakes and butter bottom layers. Spoon fruit mixture between layers and on top. Serve warm.

For 8-inch hot-milk sponge cake:

Sift together 1 cup sifted all-purpose flour, 1 teaspoon baking powder, and 1/4 teaspoon salt. Beat 2 eggs till thick and lemon-colored, about 3 minutes at high speed on electric mixer. Gradually add 1 cup sugar, beating constantly at medium speed 4 to 5 minutes. By hand, quickly fold dry ingredients into egg mixture. Add 2 tablespoons butter to 1/2 cup *hot* milk; stir with 1 teaspoon vanilla into batter; blend well. Pour into paper-lined 8x8x2-inch baking pan. Bake at 350° for 25 to 30 minutes. Cool cake in pan for 15 minutes; remove from pan; cool. Cut in squares to serve. Top with fruit and ice cream.

SHORTCAKE FILLINGS

Strawberry:

Layer shortcake with sweetened sliced fresh strawberries and whipped or ice cream.

Strawberry-rhubarb:

Combine 3 cups 1-inch pieces fresh rhubarb, 3/4 cup sugar, dash salt, and 1/2 cup water in saucepan. Bring to boil; reduce heat and cook covered 5 minutes. Blend 1 1/2 tablespoons cornstarch and 3 tablespoons water; stir into rhubarb. Cook, stirring constantly, till mixture boils. Reduce heat; cook and stir 2 minutes. Cool. Stir in 3 cups sliced fresh strawberries. Serve on biscuit with whipped cream.

Rhubarb:

Combine 4 cups diced fresh rhubarb, 1 cup sugar, dash salt, and 3/4 cup water. Bring to boil; reduce heat; cook covered about 10 minutes. Blend 2 tablespoons cornstarch and 1/4 cup water; stir into rhubarb. Cook, stirring constantly, till mixture boils. Reduce heat; cook and stir 2 minutes. Cool. Fill and top shortcake with rhubarb and whipped cream.

Cranberry-banana:

Combine 1 cup sugar and 1/2 cup water in saucepan; stir till dissolved. Bring to boil; boil 5 minutes. Add 1/2 pound (2 cups) cranberries and cook till skins pop, about 5 minutes. Remove from heat. Stir in 2 sliced bananas. Serve on biscuit with whipped cream.

Peach:

Dip 1 quart fresh sliced peaches in lemon juice. Sweeten. Whip 1 cup whipping cream with 2 tablespoons brown sugar. Fold *half* the peaches into *half* the cream. Spread on bottom layer of biscuit. Cover top half of biscuit with remaining peaches and cream.

Old-fashioned Shortcake—plump, juicy →
strawberries nestled on a warm, rich biscuit with fluffy mounds of whipped cream.

Cake-bakers' specialties

PEACH PRESERVE CAKE

½ cup butter or margarine
1 cup sugar
½ cup peach preserves
2 eggs
2 cups sifted all-purpose flour
2 teaspoons baking powder
¼ teaspoon soda
1 teaspoon salt
½ teaspoon ground cinnamon
1 teaspoon grated orange peel
½ cup orange juice
Peach Frosting

Cream first 3 ingredients thoroughly. Add eggs; beat till fluffy. Sift together dry ingredients. Add to creamed mixture alternately with the combined orange peel, juice, and ¼ cup water; beat after each addition. Bake in greased and lightly floured 13x9x2-inch pan at 350° about 35 minutes or till done. Cool. Frost top with *Peach Frosting:* Cream ¼ cup butter with ⅓ cup peach preserves. Gradually add 2 cups sifted confectioners' sugar; beat frosting till light and fluffy.

BANANA PRUNE CAKE

Place ⅔ cup shortening in bowl. Sift together 2¼ cups sifted all-purpose flour, 1½ cups sugar, 1½ teaspoons baking powder, ½ teaspoon soda, and 1 teaspoon salt. Add to shortening with 1 cup (2 to 3) mashed ripe bananas and ⅓ cup milk; mix till all flour is moistened. Beat vigorously 2 minutes. Add 2 eggs and ⅓ cup milk; beat 2 minutes longer. Fold in 1 cup pitted cooked prunes, finely snipped, and ½ cup chopped California walnuts. Turn into greased and lightly floured 13x9x2-inch pan. Bake at 350° about 45 to 50 minutes or till done.

When cool, frost with *Brown Sugar Frosting:* Place 1 egg white, ¾ cup brown sugar, 3 tablespoons cold water, and dash salt in top of double boiler. Beat 1 minute with electric mixer. Cook over boiling water, beating constantly till mixture forms peaks, about 3 to 4 minutes. Remove from heat. Add 1 teaspoon vanilla and beat to spreading consistency.

ORANGE BLOSSOM CAKE

1 medium orange
1 package 2-layer-size yellow cake mix
1½ cups sugar
3 tablespoons cornstarch
¼ teaspoon salt
¼ cup butter or margarine
1 cup water
1 3½-ounce can flaked coconut
1 package fluffy white frosting mix

Cut unpeeled orange in chunks; blend at low speed in electric blender till almost smooth, or put through food chopper, using fine blade (⅔ cup ground orange will be needed).

Prepare cake mix following package directions; fold ⅓ *cup* of the ground orange into batter. Bake according to directions in 2 greased and floured 8x1½-inch round pans. Cool 5 minutes. Remove from pans; cool.

Combine sugar, next 4 ingredients, and remaining ground orange. Cook and stir till mixture thickens and boils; cook 2 minutes. Cool; stir in coconut. Split each cake layer once, making 4 layers. Spread layers and top of cake with orange-coconut filling. Prepare frosting mix according to directions; spread on sides of cake. Trim with orange sections.

STRAWBERRY CRUNCH CAKE

Sift together 2 cups sifted all-purpose flour, 4 teaspoons baking powder, ⅓ cup sugar, and ¾ teaspoon salt; cut in ⅓ cup shortening. Combine ⅔ cup milk and 1 slightly beaten egg; stir into flour mixture; blend well. Spread in greased 11x7x1½-inch pan.

Spoon 2 cups sliced fresh strawberries over batter; sprinkle with ½ cup sugar. Mix ¼ cup softened butter or margarine, ¼ cup sugar, and ⅓ cup all-purpose flour; crumble over berries. Bake at 425° for 35 to 40 minutes. Serve warm with ice cream. Serves 8.

Orange Blossom Cake has bits of fresh → orange scattered throughout the mix-easy cake as well as in the ambrosial filling.

ALMOND PEACH TORTE

Combine 2½ cups sifted all-purpose flour, ½ cup finely chopped toasted almonds, ⅓ cup sugar, and ½ teaspoon salt; cut in ¾ cup butter. Gradually add ⅓ cup cold water; gently toss with fork to moisten. Form dough in ball; divide dough in thirds. Roll each third on ungreased baking sheet to ⅛-inch thickness; trim to 8-inch circles. Bake in a moderate oven (375°) till lightly browned, 10 to 12 minutes; cool.

Drain and chill one 1-pound 14-ounce can sliced peaches and one 8¾-ounce can crushed pineapple. Whip 2 cups whipping cream with ¼ cup sugar and ¼ teaspoon almond extract; set aside 1½ cups for frosting. Reserving 6 peach slices, chop remaining and fold with pineapple into whipped cream. To assemble, spread half the mixture on one crust, top with second crust, remaining filling and third crust. Frost with reserved whipped cream. Garnish with reserved peaches and 2 table-spoons toasted slivered almonds. Serves 8 to 10.

PRUNE SPICE CAKE

  ½ pound (1½ cups) dried prunes
  2 cups sifted all-purpose flour
1½ cups sugar
1¼ teaspoons soda
  1 teaspoon salt
  1 teaspoon ground cinnamon
  1 teaspoon ground nutmeg
  ¼ to ½ teaspoon ground cloves
  ½ cup salad oil
  3 eggs
    Crumb Topping
  ½ cup broken California walnuts

Cover prunes with water. Cover and simmer 30 minutes or till tender. (Do not sweeten.) Drain, reserving ⅔ cup of the liquid (add water, if necessary). Pit and chop prunes.

Sift together dry ingredients; add reserved prune liquid and salad oil. Mix to blend. Beat vigorously 2 minutes. Add eggs; beat 1 minute. Stir in prunes. Pour into greased and floured 13x9x2-inch baking dish. Sprinkle with Crumb Topping, then nuts. Bake at 350° about 35 minutes. Serve warm.

Crumb Topping: Mix ½ cup sugar and 2 tablespoons all-purpose flour; cut in 2 table-spoons butter or margarine till crumbly.

EASY PLUM PUDDING

  1 1-pound 1-ounce jar (2 cups) purple plums
  1 package gingerbread mix
  ½ teaspoon salt
  1 cup light raisins
  ½ cup chopped California walnuts
  ¼ cup sugar
  2 tablespoons cornstarch
  1 tablespoon lemon juice
    Fluffy Hard Sauce

Drain plums, reserving syrup for sauce. Remove pits and cut plums in pieces. Prepare gingerbread mix according to package directions, adding salt and plum pieces. Stir in raisins and nuts. Turn batter into well-greased 6-cup mold*. Bake, uncovered, in moderate oven (375°) about 1 hour. Loosen edges and immediately unmold on plate.

*Or, pour batter into 12 well-greased 5-ounce custard cups. Arrange cups in large shallow baking pan. Cover each with foil and bake at 375° about 40 minutes.

Meanwhile, prepare *Plum Sauce:* Add water to reserved plum syrup to make 1½ cups. Combine sugar and cornstarch in small saucepan. Gradually stir in plum syrup. Cook, over medium heat, stirring constantly, till mixture thickens and boils; cook and stir 1 minute more. Stir in lemon juice. Serve warm over plum pudding; pass Fluffy Hard Sauce.

Fluffy Hard Sauce: Thoroughly cream together ½ cup butter or margarine and 2 cups sifted confectioners' sugar. Stir in 1 beaten egg yolk and 1 teaspoon vanilla. Fold in 1 stiffly beaten egg white. Chill. Serves 10 to 12.

CHIP-CHERRY FRUITCAKE

Beat 3 eggs; stir in 1 cup sugar. Sift together 1½ cups sifted all-purpose flour, 1½ tea-spoons baking powder, and ¼ teaspoon salt; combine with one 6-ounce package (1 cup) semisweet chocolate pieces, 2 cups chopped pecans, one 8-ounce package dates, coarsely snipped (1⅓ cups), and 1 cup halved candied cherries. Fold in egg-sugar mixture. Turn into greased and paper-lined 9x5x3-inch loaf pan. Place pan of water on bottom oven rack while baking. Bake on top rack at 325° for 1 hour. Cool slightly; remove from pan; cool on rack. Makes 1 large cake.

Easy Plum Pudding with Fluffy Hard Sauce,
Chip-Cherry Fruitcake, and miniature Fruitcake Bonbons are all festive holiday desserts.

FRUITCAKE BONBONS

　　1　6-ounce can frozen orange juice
　　　　concentrate, thawed
　½　cup molasses
　　1　15-ounce package (3 cups) raisins
　　1　1-pound jar (2 cups) mixed
　　　　chopped candied fruits and peels
　½　cup butter or margarine
　⅔　cup sugar
　　3　eggs
1¼　cups sifted all-purpose flour
　⅛　teaspoon soda
　　1　teaspoon ground cinnamon
　½　teaspoon ground nutmeg
　¼　teaspoon ground allspice
　¼　teaspoon ground cloves
　½　cup chopped California walnuts

In saucepan, combine first 3 ingredients.
Cook over medium heat, stirring occasionally
till mixture comes to boiling. Reduce heat;
simmer 5 minutes; remove from heat. Reserving ½ cup candied fruit, stir in remainder.

Cream butter and sugar together. Beat in
eggs, one at a time. Sift together dry ingredients. Stir into creamed mixture. Add
orange juice mixture and nuts; mix well.

Line 1¾-inch muffin pans with miniature
paper bake cups. Place 1 tablespoon batter in
each; top with 1 or 2 pieces of reserved fruit.
Bake at 350° for 20 to 25 minutes. Cool;
wrap; tie. Makes 90 tiny cakes.

Or, line one 11x4x3-inch pan and two 5½x
3x2¼-inch pans with heavy paper, allowing
½ inch to extend above all sides. Spoon batter
into pans, filling about ¾ full. Bake at 275°
about 2¼ to 2½ hours for large loaf and
about 1½ hours for smaller loaves. Cool
cakes in pans; remove. Wrap in foil or clear
plastic wrap and store in cool place several
weeks. Makes about 3½ pounds fruitcake.

APPLE RAISIN CAKE

- ½ cup butter or margarine
- 2 cups sugar
- 2 eggs

. . .

- 2½ cups sifted all-purpose flour
- 1½ teaspoons soda
- 1 teaspoon salt
- 1 teaspoon ground cinnamon
- ½ teaspoon ground nutmeg
- ¼ teaspoon ground allspice
- 1½ cups canned applesauce
- ½ cup raisins
- ½ cup chopped pecans
  Orange Butter Frosting

Cream butter and sugar till fluffy. Add eggs, one at a time, beating well after each. Sift together dry ingredients. Add alternately to creamed mixture with applesauce. Stir in raisins and nuts. Turn batter into greased and lightly floured 13x9x2-inch baking pan. Bake in moderate oven (350°) about 45 minutes or till done. Cool in pan.

Frost with *Orange Butter Frosting:* Cream 6 tablespoons butter or margarine with 1 teaspoon grated orange peel and dash salt. Beat in 3 cups sifted confectioners' sugar and enough orange juice (about 3 tablespoons) to make of spreading consistency.

BANANA CAKE

- ⅔ cup shortening
- 2½ cups sifted cake flour
- 1⅔ cups sugar
- 1¼ teaspoons baking powder
- 1 teaspoon soda
- 1 teaspoon salt
- 1¼ cups mashed fully ripe bananas
- ⅔ cup buttermilk *or* sour milk
- 2 eggs

Place shortening in mixing bowl. Sift dry ingredients together; add to shortening. Add mashed bananas and ⅓ *cup* buttermilk; mix till moistened. Beat vigorously 2 minutes. Add remaining buttermilk and eggs; beat 2 minutes longer. Bake in 2 greased and lightly floured 8x1½-inch round pans in moderate oven (350°) about 40 minutes or till done. Cool 10 minutes; remove from pans. Cool. Frost with a creamy butter-type frosting.

ORANGE SPONGE CAKE

- 6 egg yolks
- 1 tablespoon grated orange peel
- ½ cup orange juice
- 1 cup sugar
- ¼ teaspoon salt
- 1⅓ cups sifted cake flour
- 6 egg whites
- 1 teaspoon cream of tartar
- ½ cup sugar

Beat yolks till thick and lemon-colored. Add peel and juice; beat till very thick. Gradually add 1 cup sugar and salt; beat well. Carefully fold in flour. Beat egg whites and cream of tartar till soft peaks form. Gradually add ½ cup sugar, beating to stiff peaks. Fold whites into yolk mixture. Bake in *ungreased* 10-inch tube pan at 325° about 55 minutes, or till done. Invert; cool.

PINEAPPLE DELIGHT CAKE

Prepare and bake 1 package 2-layer-size yellow cake mix in two 9x1½-inch round pans following package directions; cool. Stir one 3¾- or 3⅝-ounce package *instant* vanilla pudding mix (dry) into one 13½-ounce can (1⅔ cups) crushed pineapple (undrained). Prepare one 2-ounce package dessert topping mix according to package directions; fold in pineapple mixture. Frost and fill cake layers. Garnish sides and top with halved pineapple slices and maraschino cherries. Chill till serving time.

CHOCOLATE DATE CAKE

- 1¼ cups boiling water
- ½ pound (1½ cups) snipped dates
- 1 package 2-layer-size chocolate cake mix
- 1 6-ounce package (1 cup) semi-sweet chocolate pieces
- ½ cup chopped California walnuts

Pour water over dates; cool. Prepare cake mix following package directions, substituting date mixture for liquid. Turn into greased and floured 13x9x2-inch pan. Top with chocolate and nuts. Bake at 350° for 35 to 40 minutes. Serve with ice cream.

Warm fruit fancies

BLUEBERRY SHORTCAKE

2 cups sifted all-purpose flour
2 tablespoons sugar
2½ teaspoons baking powder
½ teaspoon salt
½ cup butter or margarine
1 slightly beaten egg
½ cup milk
1 cup fresh blueberries
Blueberry Sauce

Sift together flour, sugar, baking powder, and salt; cut in butter. Mix egg and milk; stir into flour mixture. Divide the dough in half. Pat *half* into greased 8x1½-inch round cake pan; top with blueberries.

On waxed paper, roll remaining dough to an 8-inch circle. Invert and fit dough over berries; remove paper; sprinkle dough with 2 teaspoons sugar. Bake in hot oven (400°) for 25 to 30 minutes. Cut in 6 wedges.

Serve with warm *Blueberry Sauce:* In saucepan, combine ¼ cup sugar and 1½ tablespoons cornstarch; blend in 1 cup cold water. Cook and stir till mixture boils. Add 1 cup blueberries; cook 3 minutes. Remove from heat; stir in 1 tablespoon lemon juice and ¼ cup butter or margarine. Serves 6.

CHERRY COCONUT DELIGHT

½ cup butter or margarine
¾ cup brown sugar
1 cup sifted all-purpose flour
1 3½-ounce can (1⅓ cups) flaked coconut
⅔ cup fine saltine cracker crumbs (about 14 crackers)
1 1-pound 5-ounce can cherry pie filling

In saucepan, melt butter. Blend in sugar, flour, coconut, and crumbs; mix well. Press *half* the mixture firmly into 8x8x2-inch baking dish. Spread with cherry pie filling. Add remaining crumbs atop, pressing gently.

Bake in moderate oven (350°) for 30 minutes or till golden brown. Serve with scoops of vanilla ice cream. Makes 6 to 8 servings.

DATE PUDDING CAKE

1 cup pitted dates, cut up
1 cup boiling water
½ cup granulated sugar
½ cup brown sugar
1 egg
2 tablespoons butter or margarine, melted
1½ cups sifted all-purpose flour
1 teaspoon soda
½ teaspoon baking powder
½ teaspoon salt
½ cup chopped California walnuts
Brown Sugar Sauce

Combine dates and water. Blend sugars, egg, and butter. Sift together dry ingredients; add to sugar mixture. Stir in nuts and cooled date mixture. Pour into 11x7x1½-inch pan.

Top with Brown Sugar Sauce. Bake at 375° about 40 minutes. To serve, cut in squares while warm; invert on plates and top with vanilla ice cream. Serves 9 to 12.

Brown Sugar Sauce: Combine 1½ cups brown sugar, 1 tablespoon butter or margarine, and 1½ cups boiling water.

COCONUT APPLE SQUARES

½ cup butter or margarine, softened
½ cup brown sugar
1 teaspoon vanilla
1½ cups sifted all-purpose flour
¼ teaspoon salt
1 3½-ounce can (1⅓ cups) flaked coconut
1 1-pound 5-ounce can apple pie filling
1 tablespoon lemon juice
½ teaspoon ground cinnamon
¼ teaspoon ground mace

Cream first 3 ingredients. Sift together flour and salt; add to creamed mixture. Add coconut; mix. Pat *half* in greased 8x8x2-inch pan. Mix remaining ingredients; spoon over first layer; pat remaining coconut mixture atop. Bake at 375° for 20 to 25 minutes. Serve warm with ice cream. Serves 9.

QUICK APPLESAUCE CRISP

    1 1-pound can (2 cups)
         applesauce
    ½ cup brown sugar
    ¼ cup raisins
    ½ teaspoon ground cinnamon
    1 cup packaged biscuit mix
    ½ cup granulated sugar
    ¼ cup butter or margarine
    ¼ cup chopped California walnuts

Combine first 4 ingredients; pour into a 8¼x 1¾-inch round baking dish. Combine biscuit mix and granulated sugar; cut in butter till crumbly. Add walnuts; sprinkle over applesauce mixture. Bake in moderate oven (375°) 30 to 35 minutes. Serve warm. Serves 6.

CHERRY COOKIE CRISP

    1 1-pound can (2 cups) pitted tart
         red cherries (water pack)
    1 teaspoon lemon juice
         Red food coloring
    ⅓ cup sugar
    ½ teaspoon ground cinnamon
    1½ cups vanilla wafer crumbs
    ⅓ cup butter or margarine,
         melted

Drain cherries, reserving 2 tablespoons juice. Mix cherries, reserved juice, lemon juice, and few drops food coloring. Pour into 10x6x1½-inch baking dish. Mix sugar and cinnamon; sprinkle over. Mix crumbs and butter; pat over cherries. Bake in hot oven (400°) 25 minutes or till done. Serve warm. Serves 6.

RHUBARB CRUNCH

Combine 4 cups rhubarb cut in 1-inch pieces, ½ cup granulated sugar, 1 tablespoon flour, and 1 teaspoon shredded orange peel; turn into 8¼x1¾-inch round baking dish.

For topping, combine ¾ cup all-purpose flour, ¾ cup brown sugar, and dash salt. Cut in ¼ cup butter or margarine till crumbly. Sprinkle over rhubarb. Bake at 350° for 40 to 45 minutes. Serve warm. Combine ½ cup dairy sour cream, 2 tablespoons confectioners' sugar, and ½ teaspoon vanilla; spoon atop each serving. Makes 6 servings.

FIG-NUT SQUARES

    ½ cup butter or margarine
    1¾ cups brown sugar
    4 well beaten eggs
    1 teaspoon grated lemon peel
    1 teaspoon grated orange peel
    2 cups snipped dried figs or
         dates
    1 cup chopped California walnuts
    1½ cups sifted all-purpose flour
    1 teaspoon baking powder
    ½ teaspoon salt
         Creamy Hard Sauce

Melt butter; stir in brown sugar. Add eggs; mix well. Stir in lemon and orange peel, *half* the figs, and *half* the nuts. Sift together dry ingredients. Blend into batter. Pour into greased 13x9x2-inch baking pan. Sprinkle with remaining figs and nuts. Bake in slow oven (325°) for 50 to 55 minutes.

Serve warm with softened ice cream or with *Creamy Hard Sauce:* Thoroughly cream together ¼ cup butter or margarine and 2 cups sifted confectioners' sugar. Add 3 tablespoons milk and 1 teaspoon vanilla; mix well. Whip ½ cup whipping cream; fold into creamed mixture. Pass with fig squares. Serves 12.

APPLE SOUR-CREAM BAKE

    1½ cups sifted all-purpose flour
    ½ cup sugar
    2 teaspoons baking powder
    ½ teaspoon salt
    ½ teaspoon ground cinnamon
    ½ cup milk
    ¼ cup butter or margarine,
         softened
    1 egg
    1 cup diced pared tart apples
    ½ cup dairy sour cream
    1 slightly beaten egg
    ¼ cup sugar
    ⅓ cup chopped California walnuts

Sift together dry ingredients. Add milk, butter, and unbeaten egg; beat till smooth. Add apples. Pour into greased 9x9x2-inch baking pan. Blend sour cream and slightly beaten egg; spread over batter. Top with mixture of sugar and walnuts. Bake at 375° for 30 minutes. Serve warm. Makes 8 or 9 servings.

LEMON CRISP

  6 tablespoons butter or margarine
  ¾ cup brown sugar
  1 cup sifted all-purpose flour
  ½ teaspoon soda
  ½ teaspoon salt
  ½ cup flaked coconut
  ¾ cup fine saltine cracker crumbs
     (about 18 crackers)
  ¾ cup granulated sugar
  2 tablespoons cornstarch
  ¼ teaspoon salt
  2 beaten egg yolks
  ½ teaspoon grated lemon peel
  ½ cup lemon juice

Cream butter and brown sugar; stir in flour, soda, ½ teaspoon salt, coconut, and crumbs. Press *half* the mixture into 8x8x2-inch baking pan. Bake at 350° for 10 minutes.

Meanwhile, in saucepan, combine granulated sugar, cornstarch, and ¼ teaspoon salt; gradually stir in 1 cup hot water. Cook and stir till mixture thickens and boils; boil about 2 minutes. Remove from heat.

Stir small amount of hot mixture into egg yolks; return to remaining mixture in pan. Bring to boil, stirring constantly; remove from heat. Gradually stir in peel and juice. Pour over baked crust; add reserved crumbs atop. Bake at 350° for 30 minutes or till golden. Pass whipped cream. Serves 8.

HONEY RHUBARB BETTY

  1 pound rhubarb, cut in ½-inch
     slices (about 4 cups)
  ¾ cup sugar
  1 teaspoon ground nutmeg
     Dash salt
  2 tablespoons water
  6 tablespoons butter or margarine,
     melted
  ½ cup honey
  5 slices bread, cut in cubes (about
     4 cups)

Combine rhubarb, sugar, nutmeg, salt, and water in 10x6x1½-inch baking dish. Blend butter and honey; stir in bread cubes. Spoon evenly over top of rhubarb. Bake in moderate oven (375°) about 30 minutes, or till topping is light golden brown. Makes 4 to 6 servings.

ORANGE CHIFFON SOUFFLE

  ¼ cup butter or margarine
  ⅓ cup all-purpose flour
     Dash salt
  1 cup milk
  1 teaspoon grated orange peel
  ½ cup orange juice
  6 egg yolks
  6 egg whites
  ¼ cup sugar
     Orange Sauce

Melt butter; blend in flour and dash salt. Add milk all at once. Cook quickly, stirring constantly, till mixture thickens and bubbles. Remove from heat; stir in orange peel and juice. Beat egg yolks till thick and lemon-colored, about 5 minutes. Slowly add orange mixture to egg yolks, stirring constantly.

Beat egg whites to soft peaks. Gradually add sugar, beating to stiff peaks. Carefully fold yolk mixture into egg whites. Pour into ungreased 2-quart souffle dish with collar.* Bake at 325° for 1 hour and 15 minutes or till knife inserted off center comes out clean.

Serve with *Orange Sauce:* In medium saucepan combine ½ cup sugar, 2 tablespoons cornstarch, and dash salt. Stir in 1½ cups orange juice. Cook and stir over low heat till mixture thickens and boils. Remove from heat; add 1 tablespoon butter and diced sections of 1 orange. Serve warm. Serves 8 to 10.

*To make collar: Measure aluminum foil to go around top of souffle dish, with 1-inch overlap; fold in thirds lengthwise; butter thoroughly. Extend collar 2 inches above top of dish; fasten with pins or tape.

HAWAIIAN FRUIT CRUMBLE

Toss 2 cups sliced pared tart apples with 1 tablespoon lemon juice; place in 10x6x1½-inch baking dish. Spoon one 8¾-ounce can (1 cup) crushed pineapple, drained, evenly over apples; then cover with one 1-pound can (2 cups) whole cranberry sauce.

For topping, mix 1 cup quick-cooking rolled oats, ¾ cup brown sugar, ½ cup all-purpose flour, ½ teaspoon ground cinnamon, and dash salt; cut in ⅓ cup butter or margarine till crumbly. Sprinkle over fruit. Bake in moderate oven (350°) for 30 minutes or till apples are tender. Serve warm. Serves 6.

The basket brims with tart Baldwin and crisp MacIntosh apples—both great for eating out of hand or tucking inside Apple Dumplings.

APPLE DUMPLINGS

Molded hard sauce or hot maple syrup accompanies these dumplings. Another time serve with wedges of sharp Cheddar cheese or pass a pitcher of cream—

    2¼ cups sifted all-purpose flour
    ½ teaspoon salt
    ⅔ cup shortening, chilled
    6 to 8 tablespoons cold water
    6 small apples, pared and cored
    ⅔ cup sugar
    ¼ cup light cream
    ¾ cup *hot* maple or maple-blended
       syrup
    6 tablespoons butter or margarine,
       softened
    1 cup sifted confectioners' sugar *or*
    1 cup brown *or* maple sugar

Mix flour and salt. Cut in shortening till mixture resembles coarse crumbs. Sprinkle water over a little at a time; mix lightly till all is moistened. Form into ball; roll out on lightly floured surface to 18x12-inch rectangle; cut into six 6-inch squares.

Place an apple in center of each square. Mix granulated sugar and cream; spoon into centers of apples. Moisten edges of pastry; fold corners to center; pinch edges together.

Place 1 inch apart in ungreased 11x7x1½-inch baking pan. Bake in very hot oven (450°) for 15 minutes. Reduce oven temperature to 350°. Baste apples with hot maple syrup. Return to oven and bake 30 minutes longer or till apples are done, basting with hot maple syrup every 15 minutes.

Serve with additional hot maple syrup or *Hard Sauce:* Cream butter with confectioners' sugar till fluffy. Drop from teaspoon onto waxed paper, making 6 mounds. Sprinkle generously with nutmeg; chill. Serves 6.

PEACH-CHEESE DUMPLINGS

  1 1-pound 13-ounce can
     peach halves
1½ cups sifted all-purpose flour
  ¾ teaspoon salt
  ½ cup shortening
  ½ cup shredded sharp process
     American cheese
  3 to 4 tablespoons cold water
     Butter and ground cinnamon
     Lemon Sauce

Drain peaches, reserving 1 cup syrup. Sift flour with ¾ teaspoon salt; cut in shortening till size of small peas. Add cheese and mix lightly. Blend in water as for pastry.

Roll dough on lightly floured surface to 18x12-inch rectangle. Cut in six 6-inch squares. Place peach half, cut side down, in center of each square. Dot with butter; dash with cinnamon. Moisten edges of pastry and fold over peach, pinching to seal. Place dumplings on ungreased baking sheet. Bake at 425° for 20 to 25 minutes. Serves 6.

Serve with *Lemon Sauce:* In saucepan, blend ¼ cup sugar, 1 tablespoon cornstarch, and dash salt; gradually add 1 cup reserved peach syrup. Cook and stir till clear and thickened. Add 1 teaspoon grated lemon peel, 1 tablespoon lemon juice, 1 tablespoon butter.

BLUEBERRY SLUMP

  1 cup sifted all-purpose flour
  2 tablespoons sugar
  2 teaspoons baking powder
  ¼ teaspoon salt
  1 tablespoon butter or margarine
2½ cups fresh blueberries
  ⅓ cup sugar
     Dash salt
  1 tablespoon lemon juice
  ½ cup milk

Sift together first 4 ingredients; cut in butter till like coarse meal; set aside. Bring berries, ⅓ cup sugar, salt, and 1 cup water to boil; cover and simmer 5 minutes; add lemon juice. Add milk to dry ingredients; stir till moistened. Drop dough in 6 spoonfuls into *bubbling* sauce (don't overlap). Cover *tightly;* cook over low heat 10 minutes without peeking. Serve hot with cream. Serves 6.

ITALIAN PLUM COBBLER

1½ cups packaged biscuit mix
  2 tablespoons sugar
  2 tablespoons butter or margarine,
     melted
1½ pounds Italian plums, pitted and
     quartered (about 3½ cups)
1¼ cups sugar
  ¼ cup water
  2 tablespoons quick-cooking
     tapioca
  2 tablespoons butter or margarine
  ⅓ to ½ cup milk

Combine biscuit mix, 2 tablespoons sugar, and melted butter; set aside. Combine plums, 1¼ cups sugar, water, and tapioca. Cook over medium heat, stirring constantly, till mixture boils; stir in the 2 tablespoons butter. Pour into 8x8x2-inch pan.

Add enough milk to dry ingredients to moisten; drop by spoonfuls on top of hot plum mixture; spread atop. Bake in hot oven (425°) for 20 minutes or till done. Serve warm with plain or whipped cream. Serves 6 to 8.

SPEEDY ORANGE COBBLER

  2 cups packaged biscuit mix
  ¼ cup sugar
  ½ teaspoon ground nutmeg
  ¼ cup butter or margarine
  ¼ cup sugar
  2 tablespoons cornstarch
  ¾ cup orange marmalade
1½ cups orange juice
  2 tablespoons butter or margarine
  ½ cup orange juice

Combine biscuit mix, ¼ cup sugar, and nutmeg. Cut in ¼ cup butter till mixture resembles coarse crumbs. Set aside.

In medium saucepan, combine ¼ cup sugar, cornstarch, and marmalade. Stir in 1½ cups orange juice. Cook and stir over medium heat till mixture thickens and boils; cook 2 minutes more; stir in 2 tablespoons butter. Turn into 10x6x1½-inch baking dish.

Add ½ cup orange juice to dry ingredients; stir just till moistened. Drop dough by spoonfuls onto hot orange sauce. Bake in moderate oven (350°) for 30 minutes. Serve warm with scoops of ice cream. Makes 6 servings.

Dessert waffles, pancakes

DESSERT WAFFLES JUBILEE

2¼ cups sifted all-purpose flour
4 teaspoons baking powder
¾ teaspoon salt
1½ tablespoons sugar
2 slightly beaten egg yolks
2¼ cups milk
½ cup salad oil
2 stiffly beaten egg whites
Fluffy Cream Sauce
Cherry Topper

Sift together dry ingredients. Combine egg yolks, milk, and salad oil; stir into dry ingredients. Fold in stiffly beaten egg whites, leaving a few little fluffs—don't overmix. Bake in preheated waffle baker.

To serve: Stack 5 or 6 hot waffles on serving plate. Top each waffle with some of the Fluffy Cream Sauce and Cherry Topper. Cut in wedges. Pass extra sauces. Serves 6.

Fluffy Cream Sauce: In small mixing bowl, combine one 4-ounce package whipped cream cheese and ¼ cup sifted confectioners' sugar; whip till light and fluffy. Gradually add 1 cup whipping cream, beating till slightly fluffy but not thick. Makes 2 cups sauce.

Cherry Topper: Combine one 1-pound 5-ounce can cherry pie filling and 2 or 3 drops almond extract; heat through. Makes 2 cups.

DATE TORTE WAFFLES

1 cup packaged biscuit mix
1 cup snipped dates
½ cup chopped California walnuts
½ cup sugar
2 well beaten eggs
¼ cup milk
2 tablespoons salad oil
1 teaspoon vanilla
Vanilla ice cream

Combine biscuit mix, dates, and nuts. Add sugar to eggs; beat well. Stir in milk, oil, and vanilla; gently fold into biscuit mixture. Bake in preheated waffle baker. To serve, sandwich a scoop of ice cream between 2 hot waffles. Makes 4 servings.

SPRING PANCAKES

2 cups sifted all-purpose flour
5 teaspoons baking powder
2 teaspoons sugar
½ teaspoon salt
2 cups milk
½ cup light cream
2 beaten eggs
¼ cup butter or margarine, melted
Marshmallow Cream
Strawberry Sauce

Sift together dry ingredients. Combine milk, cream, eggs, and butter; add to dry ingredients; beat smooth. Using ⅓ cup batter, bake 6 inch pancakes on hot griddle. Keep warm in very slow oven on towel-covered pan.

To serve: Brush pancakes with melted butter; sprinkle with brown sugar (1 teaspoon each); stack on warm platter. Spoon Marshmallow Cream atop; drizzle with Strawberry Sauce; trim with berries. Serves 6.

Marshmallow Cream: Mix one 1-pint jar marshmallow creme and ¼ cup softened butter; fold in ½ cup whipping cream, whipped.

Strawberry Sauce: Reserving few berries for trim, halve or quarter 1 quart fresh strawberries; mix with ½ cup sugar; heat to boiling.

ORANGE DESSERT PANCAKES

1 beaten egg
1 cup light cream
1 6-ounce can frozen orange juice concentrate, thawed
1 cup packaged pancake mix
Orange Sauce

Combine egg, cream, and ¼ *cup* orange juice concentrate. Add pancake mix, stirring to remove most lumps. Bake on hot greased griddle. Makes 18. Serve with warm *Orange Sauce:* Mix ½ cup butter, 1 cup sugar, and remaining orange juice concentrate. Heat to boiling, stirring occasionally. Makes 1½ cups sauce.

Dessert Waffles Jubilee makes a sophisticated dessert. Glamorous topping is convenient pie filling spiked with almond.

Colorful compotes

NECTARINE GRAPE COMPOTE

8 nectarines, peeled and sliced (about 4 cups)
2 cups seedless green grapes
1 cup white grape juice
2 tablespoons orange liqueur
1 pint pineapple sherbet

In serving bowl, combine fruits. Add grape juice and liqueur; stir gently; chill. To serve, spoon into dishes; top each serving with a scoop of sherbet. Makes 8 servings.

FRUIT MEDLEY ELEGANTE

Luscious compote shown opposite contents page—

⅓ cup port
¼ cup orange juice
1 tablespoon lemon juice
2 to 3 tablespoons sugar
1 cup peeled, sliced peaches
1 cup halved strawberries
6 pear halves
1 large banana, peeled and sliced

Combine wine, fruit juices, and sugar. Pour over combined fruits; toss; chill. Serves 6.

RUBY FRUIT COMPOTE

1 1-pound 4-ounce can frozen pitted tart red cherries, thawed
1 10-ounce package frozen raspberries, thawed
1½ tablespoons cornstarch
1 tablespoon lemon juice
1 pint (2 cups) fresh whole strawberries
Dairy sour cream

Drain frozen fruits, reserving syrup. Add enough water to syrup to make 2½ cups. Blend cornstarch, dash salt, and syrup. Cook and stir till thickened and clear. Add lemon juice. Stir in fruits. Chill thoroughly. To serve, spoon into sherbets; top with a dollop of sour cream. Makes 8 servings.

BAKED AMBROSIA

Four favorite fruits with a toasty coconut topper—

1 1-pound can (2 cups) apricot halves
1 1-pound can (2 cups) peach halves
1 1-pound can (2 cups) purple plums
3 or 4 thin orange slices, halved
½ cup orange juice
¼ cup brown sugar
½ teaspoon shredded lemon peel
2 tablespoons butter or margarine, melted
½ cup flaked coconut

Drain canned fruits well; arrange with orange slices in a shallow baking dish. Mix orange juice, sugar, and peel; pour over fruit. Drizzle melted butter over the plums; sprinkle coconut over all. Bake in hot oven (425°) 15 minutes or till hot and coconut is toasted. Serve warm. Makes 8 servings.

HONEY-FRUIT COMPOTE

1 1-pound 4½-ounce can (2½ cups) pineapple slices or chunks
2 oranges, peeled and sectioned
1 teaspoon shredded orange peel
Juice of 1 orange
¼ cup honey
2 tablespoons butter or margarine
1 1-pound can (2 cups) pitted dark sweet cherries, drained
2 tablespoons orange liqueur

Drain pineapple, reserving ½ cup syrup. Arrange pineapple in shallow baking dish. Add orange sections; sprinkle with peel. Combine reserved syrup, the orange juice, and honey; pour over fruit. Dot with butter. Bake at 350° for 20 minutes, basting frequently. Add cherries; bake 10 minutes. Sprinkle with liqueur. Serve warm. Pass bowl of cinnamon-flavored dairy sour cream. Makes 6 servings.

Sparkling finale for any cool midsummer → meal—flavor-packed nectarines team with juicy grapes in Nectarine Grape Compote.

HARVEST FRUIT COMPOTE

1 1-pound package dried prunes
½ of 11-ounce package (1⅓ cups) dried apricots
1 13½-ounce can (1⅔ cups) pineapple chunks, undrained
1 1-pound 5-ounce can cherry pie filling
2 cups water
¼ cup dry sherry

In 9x9x2-inch baking dish, layer prunes, apricots, and pineapple. Combine remaining ingredients; pour over fruit. Cover and bake at 350° for 1½ hours. Serve warm. Serves 8.

HOT FRUIT COMPOTE

In 2-quart casserole, combine two 11-ounce packages mixed dried fruits, ½ cup raisins, 2 cups water, ¼ cup lemon juice, ½ cup brown sugar, 1 teaspoon cinnamon, ¼ cup butter, ½ cup soft bread crumbs, 1 teaspoon salt, and ¼ cup cream sherry or port. Cover and bake at 350° for 1½ hours, stirring several times during baking. Serve hot. Serves 6.

PEACH-COT CHERRY BAKE

1 1-pound 1-ounce can sliced peaches (undrained)
1 cup dried apricots
½ cup brown sugar
½ teaspoon grated lemon peel
2 tablespoons lemon juice
1 teaspoon grated orange peel
⅓ cup orange juice
1 1-pound can pitted dark sweet cherries, drained

In 10x6x1½-inch baking dish, mix first 7 ingredients. Cover; bake at 350° for 45 minutes. Add cherries; bake 15 minutes. Serves 8.

GOLDEN FRUIT MEDLEY

Cook ½ pound dried prunes, covered, in 3 cups water 30 minutes. Add ½ lemon, thinly sliced, 1 cup raisins, and ½ cup sugar; cook 10 minutes; cool. Drain prunes and one 1-pound can pear halves, reserving syrups; mix syrups, juice of ½ lemon, and 1½ teaspoons vanilla. Pour over fruit and 2 peeled and sectioned oranges in dish; chill. Serves 6 to 8.

HOW TO COOK DRIED FRUIT	DRIED FRUIT	COOKING TIME IN MINUTES*	SUGAR/CUP UNCOOKED FRUIT
	Apples	20 to 30	4 tablespoons per cup
	Apricots	20 to 25	3 to 4 tablespoons per cup
Rinse fruit and cover with water 1 inch above fruit in saucepan. Cover; simmer gently for time specified in chart. If desired, add sugar (amount in chart) for last 5 minutes of cooking.	Figs	40 to 45	1 tablespoon per cup
	Mixed Fruits	25 to 30	2 to 3 tablespoons per cup
	Peaches	30 to 35	3 to 4 tablespoons per cup
To plump raisins, cover with water in saucepan. Bring to boiling; remove from heat; let stand covered 5 minutes.	Pears	30 to 35	3 to 4 tablespoons per cup
	Prunes	25 to 30	2 tablespoons per cup

*Some dried fruits are processed to cut cooking time. See cooking directions on package.

Easy fruit fix-ups

FLAMING PEARS MELBA

Drain two 1-pound 13-ounce cans pear halves, reserving syrup. Place 12 pear halves, cut-side down on toweling; use remaining pears another time. *For filling:* Combine one 3-ounce package cream cheese, softened, 1 tablespoon sugar, and enough syrup for spreading. Stir in ¼ cup chopped walnuts. Spread 1 tablespoon on flat surface of each pear. Press halves together, making 6 whole pears.

For sauce: In saucepan, blend ¼ cup cold water and 1 tablespoon cornstarch; stir in one 10-ounce package frozen raspberries, thawed. Cook and stir till thick; sieve.

To serve: Preheat ¼ cup brandy; pour atop warm raspberry sauce; ignite with long match. Immediately spoon over pears. Serves 6.

DEVONSHIRE GRAPES

    3 cups seedless green grapes
    ½ cup dairy sour cream
      Creme de cacao *or* brown sugar

Wash grapes; drain well. Add sour cream; mix carefully, coating grapes well. Chill at least 2 hours. Serve in sauce dishes; pass creme de cacao or brown sugar. Serves 6.

BERRY CUP

Wash, hull, and drain 1 quart strawberries. Place in bowl; top with ¼ cup sugar. Add ½ cup orange juice; mix gently. Chill 2 hours, stirring occasionally. Serves 6.

Flaming Pears Melba—sensational effect for little effort. Crimson raspberry sauce is ladled over cream cheese and walnut stuffed pears.

SPEEDY DESSERT TIPS

• Spoon a little slightly thawed lemonade concentrate over blueberries and peaches.
• Mold lightly sweetened red raspberries in tropical-fruit-flavored gelatin; crown with a fluff of whipped cream.
• Prepare vanilla pudding mix according to package directions, and fold in dairy sour cream to taste. Spoon over sliced peaches, nectarines, berries, or mixed fruits.
• Drizzle fresh lime juice, and sugar or honey to taste, over seedless green grapes and melon balls. Top with snowy flaked coconut.
• Combine pitted dark sweet cherries with lightly sugared pineapple cubes, and top with a scoop of pineapple or lemon sherbet.
• Arrange a bowl of ripe fruit, cheese board with assorted cheeses, and tray of crackers.
• Fill peach or nectarine halves with vanilla ice cream and sweetened crushed raspberries.
• Layer sugared sliced berries with soft custard in sherbet glasses. Chill thoroughly. Top with a spoonful of dairy sour cream.
• Just before serving, pour lemon-lime carbonated beverage or ginger ale over chilled sliced plums and pears; top with lime ice.
• Serve lightly honeyed pineapple cubes in sherbets; dash with chopped candied ginger.

SPICY BAKED APPLES

    6 large baking apples
    6 slices unpared orange
    ½ cup prepared mincemeat*
    1 cup brown sugar
    1 cup water
    2 tablespoons butter or margarine
    ½ teaspoon ground cinnamon
    ½ teaspoon ground nutmeg

Core apples and pare each about ¼ of the way down. Arrange orange slices in bottom of a 10x6x1½-inch baking dish. Place an apple on each orange slice and fill centers with mincemeat. In small saucepan, combine remaining ingredients; bring to boil. Pour hot syrup around apples. Bake uncovered at 350° for 50 minutes, basting occasionally. Serve warm with cream or ice cream. Makes 6 servings.

*Or fill centers of apples with mixture of ¾ cup snipped dates, 3 tablespoons chopped California walnuts, and ½ teaspoon grated orange peel. Bake as above.

BROILER BANANA SPLITS

    2 bananas
      Lemon juice
    ¼ cup butter or margarine
    ½ cup brown sugar
    2 tablespoons light cream
    ½ cup corn flakes
      Vanilla ice cream

Split bananas in half lengthwise, then halve crosswise. Place in shallow foilware pan. Brush with lemon juice. Melt butter; stir in sugar and cream. Cook and stir till bubbly. Remove from heat; add corn flakes; spoon over bananas. Broil 5 inches from heat till bubbly (about 2 minutes). Spoon into dishes; top with scoops of ice cream. Serves 4.

FLUFFY AMBROSIA

    1 1-pound can (2 cups) fruit
      cocktail, drained
    1 fully ripe banana, peeled
      and sliced
    1 pared orange, cut in sections
    ¼ cup broken California walnuts
    ½ cup whipping cream, whipped
    1 cup miniature marshmallows
      (optional)
      Shredded or flaked coconut

Combine fruit cocktail, bananas, orange sections, nuts, whipped cream, and marshmallows. Chill about an hour. Spoon into dishes; top with coconut. Makes 4 servings.

BANANA PECAN CRUNCH

    2 tablespoons butter or margarine
    6 bananas, peeled and sliced
      crosswise
    ½ cup broken pecans
    2 tablespoons molasses
    ½ cup brown sugar
    2 tablespoons butter or margarine,
      melted

In 11x7x1½-inch baking pan, melt 2 tablespoons butter; layer bananas and nuts in pan. Drizzle with molasses. Sprinkle brown sugar and melted butter atop. Bake at 350° for 10 minutes. Serve with ice cream. Serves 6.

APPLESAUCE

Chunk-style:

Pare, core, and slice 4 medium apples. In medium saucepan, combine 1 cup water and ¼ cup sugar; bring to boil. Drop apples into bubbling syrup. Cover and simmer till tender, about 8 minutes. Stir in dash mace.

Smooth:

Pare, quarter, and core 4 medium apples. In saucepan, combine apples, ¼ to ½ cup water (depending on juiciness of apples), and 2 inches stick cinnamon. Cover and simmer till apples are tender, about 10 minutes. Remove cinnamon; mash apples to smooth consistency with potato masher. Stir in ¼ cup sugar. (To make a large quantity, don't pare apples; put cooked sauce through sieve.)

Blender:

Pare, core, and cube 4 medium apples. Put ¼ cup water and 2 tablespoons lemon juice in blender container. Add apples, ¼ cup sugar, and 1 tablespoon red cinnamon candies (or 5 or 6 drops red food coloring). Cover and blend till smooth. Serve immediately. (Or transfer applesauce to saucepan and bring to boiling to keep apples from darkening.)

MAPLE BAKED APPLES

Pare top half of 6 large tart red apples; remove cores. Place in 11x7x1½-inch baking dish. Combine 1 cup maple-flavored syrup and 2 teaspoons grated lemon peel. Pour over apples. Bake at 375° for 1 hour, basting frequently. Serve warm with cream or ice cream.

BANANAS FOSTER

Peel 6 all-yellow bananas and halve lengthwise; brush with lemon juice. In skillet, melt ¾ cup brown sugar and 6 tablespoons butter. Add bananas; cook till almost tender, about 3 minutes. Drizzle ¼ cup orange liqueur atop. Serve with ice cream. Makes 6 servings.

RHUBARB SAUCE

In saucepan, combine 3 cups rhubarb cut in 1-inch pieces, ½ to ¾ cup sugar, and ¼ cup water. Bring to boil; cover and cook over low heat till tender, 5 minutes. Makes 2 cups.

PEARS AU GRATIN

> 5 ripe pears (2 pounds), pared, cored, and cut in ½-inch slices
> ¼ cup apricot preserves
> ¼ cup dry white wine
> ½ cup dry macaroon crumbs
> 3 tablespoons butter or margarine

Overlap pear slices in layers in buttered 10x6x1½-inch baking dish. Heat preserves and put through sieve; add wine and pour over pears. Sprinkle with macaroon crumbs and dot with butter. Bake in hot oven (400°) 20 to 25 minutes or till pears are done and crumbs are lightly browned. Serve warm. Serves 4.

ORANGE SUNBURSTS

For festive occasions, cut zigzag edges around the orange shells before filling—

Cut off tops of 5 oranges; with grapefruit knife, scoop out pulp. Chop pulp; mix with ½ cup snipped dates, ¼ cup flaked coconut, and a dash aromatic bitters. Spoon into orange shells. Place in 10x6x1½-inch baking dish. Pour a little water around oranges.

Bake at 325° for 25 minutes. Top each with a marshmallow. Bake 8 to 10 minutes longer, till marshmallows are golden. Serves 5.

GREEN AND GOLD AMBROSIA

> 1 1-pound 4-ounce can pineapple chunks
> 2 large fully ripe bananas
> 3 large Temple oranges
> ½ pound seedless green grapes
> ½ cup flaked coconut
> 1 7-ounce bottle (about 1 cup) ginger ale, chilled

Drain pineapple, reserving syrup. Slice bananas on bias into pineapple syrup; drain. Peel and slice oranges, removing seeds. Wash grapes; divide in small clusters. In large serving bowl, arrange in sections, *half* the pineapple, bananas, and oranges; sprinkle with *half* the coconut. Repeat to make second layer. Mound grape clusters in center. Chill thoroughly. Just before serving, slowly pour chilled ginger ale over all. Makes 6 servings.

Chilly desserts

LEMONADE PUDDING

2 slightly beaten egg yolks
1½ cups milk
1 3- or 3¼-ounce package *regular* vanilla pudding mix
1 3-ounce package cream cheese, softened
1 6-ounce can frozen lemonade concentrate, thawed
2 egg whites
¼ cup sugar
½ cup vanilla-wafer crumbs
2 tablespoons chopped California walnuts
2 tablespoons butter or margarine, melted

Combine egg yolks and milk. Prepare pudding according to package directions, *using the egg-milk mixture as the liquid*. Add cream cheese and beat smooth with electric or rotary beater; stir in lemonade concentrate. Cover surface with waxed paper and cool 10 minutes; beat smooth again. Beat egg whites to soft peaks; gradually add sugar, beating to stiff peaks. Fold egg whites into pudding. Combine crumbs, nuts, and butter. Sprinkle *half* the crumb mixture into 6 sherbet glasses. Spoon in pudding; top with remaining crumb mixture. Chill. Makes 6 servings.

LEMON-HONEY DESSERT

1 3-ounce package lemon-flavored gelatin
1¼ cups boiling water
⅓ cup honey
1 teaspoon shredded lemon peel
3 tablespoons lemon juice
Dash salt
1 cup whipping cream, whipped
¾ cup vanilla-wafer crumbs

Dissolve gelatin in water; stir in next 4 ingredients. Chill till partially set; beat till fluffy. Fold in cream. Spread *half* the crumbs in bottom of 10x6x1½-inch dish. Spoon in gelatin mixture; top with remaining crumbs. Chill till firm. Serves 6 to 8.

SNOW PUDDING

1 envelope unflavored gelatin
¾ cup sugar
¼ teaspoon salt
1 teaspoon grated lemon peel
¼ cup lemon juice
2 egg whites
Custard Sauce
Fresh strawberries

In a small saucepan, combine the gelatin, sugar, and salt. Add ½ cup cold water; stir over low heat till gelatin dissolves. Remove from heat; add ¾ cup cold water, lemon peel and juice. Chill till partially set. Turn into large mixing bowl; add unbeaten egg whites. Beat with electric mixer till mixture begins to hold its shape. Turn into eight 5-ounce custard cups. Chill firm. Unmold in serving dish. Top with Custard Sauce and strawberry halves. Serves 6 to 8.

Custard Sauce: In top of double boiler beat 3 egg yolks or 1 whole egg plus 2 egg yolks. Add 3 tablespoons sugar and dash salt. Gradually add 1½ cups scalded milk, slightly cooled, while stirring. Cook, stirring constantly over hot, *not boiling*, water till mixture coats a metal spoon. Remove from heat; cool at once by placing pan in bowl of cold water and stirring 1 or 2 minutes. Add 1 teaspoon vanilla. Chill. Makes 1½ cups.

RASPBERRY PUDDING

Drain one 10-ounce package frozen raspberries, thawed, reserving syrup. Chill berries. Add water to syrup to make 1½ cups. In saucepan, combine one 3- or 3¼-ounce package *regular* vanilla pudding mix and 1½ cups liquid. Cook according to package directions. Cover; chill till thick, about 2 hours. Beat smooth; fold in ½ cup whipping cream, whipped. Spoon into sherbet glasses; chill 2 hours. Wreathe puddings with vanilla-wafer crumbs; top with raspberries. Serves 4 to 6.

**Delicate golden Custard Sauce is spooned →
over airy puffs of Snow Pudding. Cascades
of strawberries are the crowning touch.**

STRAWBERRY SQUARES

1 cup sifted all-purpose flour
¼ cup brown sugar
½ cup chopped California walnuts
½ cup butter or margarine, melted

• • •

2 egg whites
1 cup granulated sugar
2 cups sliced fresh strawberries*
2 tablespoons lemon juice
1 cup whipping cream, whipped

Stir together first 4 ingredients; spread evenly in shallow baking pan. Bake at 350° for 20 minutes, stirring occasionally. Sprinkle ⅔ *of the crumbs* in 13x9x2-inch baking pan. Combine egg whites, sugar, berries, and lemon juice in large bowl; with electric mixer beat at high speed to stiff peaks, about 10 minutes. Fold in whipped cream. Spoon over crumbs; top with remaining crumbs. Freeze 6 hours or overnight. Cut in squares. Trim with whole strawberries. Serves 10 to 12.

*Or use one 10-ounce package frozen strawberries, partially thawed; reduce the granulated sugar in meringue to ⅔ cup.

RASPBERRY MERINGUE

1½ cups vanilla-wafer crumbs
    (about 30 small wafers)
¼ cup butter or margarine, melted
2 tablespoons sugar
4 egg whites
½ cup sugar
1 pint red raspberries, slightly sweetened

• • •

1 2-ounce package dessert topping mix
1 tablespoon lemon juice

Combine crumbs, butter, and 2 tablespoons sugar; mix well. Press firmly in bottom of 9x9x2-inch baking pan. Beat egg whites till soft peaks form; gradually add the ½ cup sugar, beating till stiff peaks form. Swirl meringue over crumb crust; bake in a slow oven (325°) for 12 to 15 minutes; cool. Spread berries over meringue. Prepare dessert topping mix according to package directions; gently stir in lemon juice. Spread over berries; chill. Cut in squares to serve. Makes 9 servings.

FROZEN APRICOT TORTE

Combine one 1-pound 14-ounce can apricots, drained and chopped, ½ cup sugar, and 1 tablespoon lemon juice. Fold in 1 cup whipping cream, whipped. Sprinkle ½ cup soft macaroon crumbs in bottom of 1-quart refrigerator tray; spoon in mixture. Top with ½ cup soft macaroon crumbs. Freeze till firm, 5 hours. Cut in wedges. Serves 6 to 8.

LEMONDOWN FANCY

¼ cup butter or margarine
½ cup brown sugar
1½ cups wheat flakes cereal
½ cup chopped California walnuts
3 eggs
½ cup granulated sugar
1 cup whipping cream
1 teaspoon grated lemon peel
¼ cup lemon juice

Combine butter and brown sugar. Cook over low heat till mixture boils; cook 1 minute. Remove from heat; stir in cereal and nuts. Spread mixture on baking sheet; cool. Separate eggs. Beat egg whites to soft peaks; gradually add sugar; beat to stiff peaks. Beat egg yolks till thick and lemon-colored; fold into meringue. Combine remaining ingredients; beat till stiff. Fold into egg mixture. Crumble cereal-nut crunch; sprinkle 2 cups into buttered 9-inch pie pan. Spoon in filling; sprinkle with remaining crunch. Freeze firm, 8 hours. Serves 8 to 10.

CHERRY ANGEL DESSERT

8 cups ½-inch cubes angel cake
1 1-pound 5-ounce can cherry pie filling
1 3¾- or 3⅝-ounce package *instant* vanilla pudding mix
1½ cups milk
1 cup dairy sour cream

Place *half* the cake in a 9x9x2-inch pan. Reserve ⅓ cup cherry filling; spoon remainder over cake. Top with remaining cake. Combine pudding mix, milk, and sour cream; beat smooth; spoon over cake. Chill 5 hours. Cut in 9 squares. Garnish with filling. Serves 9.

Mandarin Souffle is surrounded by sweet Kinnow Mandarin Orange sections. Accompaniment is fondant-stuffed dates.

FRUIT COCKTAIL SMOOTHEE

1 3¾-ounce package strawberry-flavored whipped dessert mix
1 1-pound can fruit cocktail
1 8-ounce package cream cheese
1 2-ounce package dessert topping mix

Prepare whipped dessert mix following package directions. Drain fruit, reserving ¾ cup syrup. Add syrup to softened cream cheese; beat till smooth. Fold in whipped strawberry dessert. Prepare dessert topping mix following package directions; fold into cream cheese mixture. Chill till partially set; fold in fruit. Turn into sherbet dishes. Chill 5 to 6 hours or overnight. Makes 8 to 10 servings.

MANDARIN SOUFFLE

¼ cup sugar
1 envelope (1 tablespoon) unflavored gelatin
4 well beaten egg yolks
¾ cup tangarine *or* orange juice
2 tablespoons lemon juice
2 teaspoons grated orange peel
4 egg whites
2 tablespoons sugar
1 cup whipping cream, whipped

In a saucepan, combine the ¼ cup sugar and the gelatin; blend in egg yolks, then tangerine or orange juice, and lemon juice. Cook and stir over low heat till gelatin dissolves and mixture thickens slightly. Stir in orange peel; cool to room temperature.

Beat egg whites to soft peaks; gradually add 2 tablespoons sugar, beating to stiff peaks. Fold in gelatin mixture, then the whipped cream. Turn into a 5-cup melon mold. Chill overnight or till set. Unmold on platter. Garnish with sweetened whipped cream and mandarin orange sections. Serves 6 to 8.

PEACH SOUFFLE

1 12-ounce package frozen sliced peaches, thawed, *or* 1 cup sweetened sliced fresh peaches
1 envelope (1 tablespoon) unflavored gelatin
4 slightly beaten egg yolks
2 tablespoons lemon juice
½ teaspoon vanilla
Dash salt
4 egg whites
½ cup sugar
½ cup whipping cream, whipped

Drain peaches, reserving syrup; add water to syrup to make ¾ cup. Soften gelatin in the liquid in saucepan; add egg yolks; cook and stir over low heat till gelatin dissolves and mixture coats spoon. Stir in lemon juice, vanilla, and dash salt. Cool slightly. Finely chop peaches; stir into gelatin mixture. Beat egg whites till soft peaks form; gradually add sugar, beating till stiff peaks form. Fold into gelatin mixture; fold in whipped cream. Turn into 1½-quart souffle dish; chill. Trim with additional whipped cream. Serves 6 to 8.

Elegant Cherries Portofino is simple to make—
raspberry-flavored gelatin, cherries, and wine.
Electric mixer softens ice cream for topper.

CHERRIES PORTOFINO

  1 1-pound can (2 cups) pitted
     dark sweet cherries
  ½ cup port
  2 3-ounce packages raspberry-
     flavored gelatin
  2 cups boiling water
  1 quart vanilla ice cream, softened

Drain cherries, reserving syrup. Combine drained cherries and wine; set aside about 3 hours. Dissolve gelatin in boiling water. Drain cherries, reserving wine. Combine wine with reserved cherry juice and enough cold water to make 1½ cups. Stir into gelatin. Chill till partially set. Stir in the cherries. Pour into 12x7½x2-inch dish. Chill till firm. Cut into cubes; spoon into sherbet glasses. Just before serving, top with softened ice cream. Serve with sugar cookies. Makes 8 servings.

FROSTY CRANBERRY LOAF

  1 3-ounce package cream cheese,
     softened
  ¼ cup sugar
     Dash salt
  1 cup whipping cream, whipped
     • • •
  1 1-pound can (2 cups) whole
     cranberry sauce
  ½-inch-thick slices angel cake

Combine softened cheese, sugar, and dash salt; beat till fluffy; fold in whipped cream.

Break up cranberry sauce with a spoon; fold into cream mixture. Spoon *half* this mixture over bottom of 8½x4½x2½-inch loaf dish. Arrange cake slices, in a single layer, over cranberry mixture (trim cake, if necessary, to fit dish). Repeat layers once. Freeze firm, about 8 hours. Slice to serve. Serves 8.

JEWEL SQUARES

1 1-pound 4½-ounce can (2½ cups) crushed pineapple
1 3-ounce package strawberry-flavored gelatin
1 cup boiling water
2 tablespoons lemon juice
1 cup whipping cream
2 tablespoons sugar
½ teaspoon vanilla
⅓ cup chopped California walnuts
18 graham-cracker squares
Canned pineapple tidbits

Drain crushed pineapple, reserving syrup. For top layer, dissolve gelatin in boiling water; add syrup and lemon juice. Chill till partially set. For cream layer, whip cream with sugar and vanilla; fold in crushed pineapple and nuts. For crust, line bottom of 8x8x2-inch dish with 9 graham crackers; spread with cream layer. Gently press remaining crackers atop. Arrange pineapple tidbits on each cracker. Spoon gelatin over. Chill firm. Top with whipped cream. Cut between crackers. Makes 9 servings.

PINEAPPLE FLUFF DESSERT

1¼ cups vanilla-wafer crumbs
¼ cup chopped walnuts
¼ cup butter or margarine, melted
1 1-pound 4½-ounce can (2½ cups) crushed pineapple
1 3-ounce package lemon-flavored gelatin
4 slightly beaten egg yolks
2 tablespoons butter or margarine
4 egg whites
¼ teaspoon salt
½ cup sugar

Mix crumbs, nuts, and melted butter; *reserve ¼ cup mixture*. Press remainder in bottom of 10x6x1½-inch dish; chill. Mix pineapple (with syrup), gelatin, and egg yolks; cook and stir till mixture thickens slightly. Stir in 2 tablespoons butter. Chill till partially set. Beat egg whites with salt to soft peaks; gradually add sugar, beating to stiff peaks. Fold into pineapple mixture. Pour over crust; sprinkle with reserved crumbs. Chill till set. Cut in squares. Serves 6.

BLUEBERRY RICE BAVARIAN

1 envelope (1 tablespoon) unflavored gelatin
⅓ cup sugar
Dash salt
½ cup water
1 7-ounce bottle (about 1 cup) lemon-lime carbonated beverage
1 tablespoon lemon juice
1½ cups cooked long-grain rice
1 cup whipping cream, whipped
2 cups fresh blueberries *or well-drained* frozen blueberries

In saucepan, combine gelatin, sugar, and dash salt. Add water; heat and stir till gelatin dissolves; remove from heat; cool. Stir in carbonated beverage, lemon juice, and cooked long-grain rice. Chill till partially set. Carefully fold in whipped cream and blueberries. Spoon into sherbet glasses; chill till set. Makes 8 servings.

(This dessert is also good with fresh nectarines, or fresh or drained frozen peaches.)

FRUITED CHEESECAKE

1 cup graham-cracker crumbs
¼ cup sugar
¼ cup butter or margarine, melted
• • •
1 envelope (1 tablespoon) unflavored gelatin
½ cup sugar
1 6-ounce can (⅔ cup) frozen lemonade concentrate, thawed
1½ cups cream-style cottage cheese
1 teaspoon vanilla
1 cup whipping cream, whipped
1 1-pound can (2 cups) fruit cocktail, drained

Combine crumbs and ¼ cup sugar; stir in butter. Press on bottom and sides of an 8- or 9-inch spring-form pan; chill. Combine gelatin and ½ cup sugar; stir in concentrate. Cook and stir till gelatin is dissolved; cool. Beat cottage cheese till smooth; stir in gelatin mixture and vanilla. Chill till partially set. Fold in remaining ingredients. Spoon into crust. Chill 6 to 8 hours or overnight. Garnish with additional fruit cocktail, if desired. Makes 10 to 12 servings.

Ice cream tempters

STRAWBERRY ICE CREAM

½ cup sugar
½ envelope (1½ *teaspoons*) unflavored gelatin
4 cups light cream
1 slightly beaten egg
1 teaspoon vanilla
    Dash salt
1 quart fresh strawberries
¾ cup sugar

Combine first 2 ingredients. Add *half* the cream. Stir over low heat till gelatin dissolves. Slowly stir a small amount of hot mixture into egg; mix well. Return to remaining hot mixture; cook and stir till mixture thickens slightly (about 1 minute). Chill. Add remaining cream, vanilla, and dash salt. Crush berries with ¾ cup sugar and add to the chilled mixture. Freeze in ice cream freezer according to manufacturer's directions. Let ripen about 4 hours. Makes about 2 quarts.

PEACH ICE CREAM

Prepare Strawberry Ice Cream, substituting 3 cups mashed peaches for crushed strawberries. Stir in ¼ teaspoon almond extract. Add to chilled mixture. Freeze.

CHERRY ICE CREAM

Prepare Strawberry Ice Cream, omitting sweetened strawberries. Increase sugar mixed with gelatin to ¾ cup. To chilled mixture, add ⅓ cup maraschino cherries, chopped, and 1 tablespoon cherry juice. Freeze.

SUNNY TANGERINE CREME

Fold one 6-ounce can frozen tangerine juice concentrate, thawed, into 1 cup whipping cream, whipped. Beat 2 egg whites till soft peaks form; gradually add ½ cup sugar; beat till stiff peaks form. Fold into cream. Tint with red food coloring. Pour into 1-quart refrigerator tray; freeze. Serves 6.

STRAWBERRY SHERBET

1 *teaspoon* unflavored gelatin
¾ cup sugar
    Dash salt
½ cup water
½ cup unsweetened pineapple juice
1 tablespoon lemon juice
1 quart fresh strawberries, crushed
    Meringue Shell (see Index)

Combine gelatin, sugar, and salt in saucepan. Stir in water and pineapple juice. Stir over low heat till gelatin dissolves. Remove from heat; stir in lemon juice. Chill till partially set. Stir in crushed berries; pour into 1½-quart refrigerator tray. Partially freeze; break into chunks; place in chilled bowl. Beat smooth with electric mixer; return to tray; freeze firm. Makes 1 quart.

Prepare Meringue mixture. Cover baking sheet with plain ungreased paper; draw a 9-inch circle on paper. Spread meringue over circle and shape into shell with back of spoon, making bottom about ½ inch thick and mounding around edge to make sides 2 inches high. Bake. Fill shell with sherbet. Top with marshmallow creme and berries.

RHUBARB ICE CREAM

Rosy ice cream pictured on opening dessert page—

Combine 3 cups diced fresh rhubarb, ¾ cup sugar, and 1 cup water in a saucepan. Cook, covered, 10 to 15 minutes, or till tender. Cool slightly; add 2 tablespoons lemon juice, ¼ teaspoon salt, and few drops red food coloring. Pour into 2-quart refrigerator tray. Freeze firm. Break into chunks; place in chilled bowl and beat smooth with electric mixer. Beat 2 egg whites till soft peaks form. Gradually add ¼ cup sugar, beating till stiff peaks form. Fold egg whites and 1 cup whipping cream, whipped, into rhubarb mixture. Freeze till firm in tray. Makes 2 quarts.

Strawberry Sherbet is served from a crispy → Meringue Shell and topped with fluffy marshmallow creme and strawberries.

PEACH MELBA ICE CREAM

2 cups sugar
2 envelopes unflavored gelatin
6 well beaten eggs
3 cups milk
4 cups whipping cream
2 tablespoons vanilla
1 10-ounce package frozen raspberries, thawed (undrained)
2 12-ounce packages frozen peaches,
thawed, drained, and cut up

Combine sugar and gelatin in saucepan. Add eggs and milk; cook, stirring till mixture thickens slightly. Cool to room temperature. Stir in cream, vanilla, and ½ teaspoon salt. Freeze in ice cream freezer according to manufacturer's directions till ice cream is nearly firm. Add fruits; continue freezing till firm. Let ripen. Makes about 3 quarts.

STRAWBERRY CREAM

3 slightly beaten eggs
½ cup sugar
1 15-ounce can (1⅓ cups)
sweetened condensed milk
2 cups light cream
2 10-ounce bottles strawberry-
flavored carbonated beverage
1 10-ounce package frozen strawberries, thawed
1 teaspoon vanilla

Combine all ingredients; mix thoroughly. Freeze in ice cream freezer according to manufacturer's directions. Let ripen. Garnish with fresh strawberries. Makes 2 quarts.

THREE-FRUIT SHERBET

1 ripe banana
⅓ cup frozen orange juice concentrate, slightly thawed
1 13½-ounce can frozen pineapple
chunks, cut in pieces
½ cup whipping cream

Combine all ingredients in blender container. Switch blender on and off till mixture is well blended. Pile into refrigerator tray; freeze till firm. Serve in sherbet glasses.

APRICOT FROST

1 1-pound 14-ounce can apricot
halves
1 3-ounce package orange-
flavored gelatin
1½ cups sugar
3 slightly beaten egg yolks
⅓ cup lemon juice
2 cups milk
1 cup light cream
3 stiffly beaten egg whites

Drain apricots, reserving 1 cup syrup. Mix gelatin, sugar, syrup, and egg yolks. Heat, stirring till mixture comes to boil. Remove from heat. Sieve apricots; add to gelatin. Add lemon juice. Stir in milk and cream. Freeze firm in refrigerator trays. Break in chunks; beat smooth. Fold in egg whites. Freeze firm in trays. Makes 2½ quarts.

EASY ORANGE SHERBET

In saucepan, mix one 3-ounce package orange-flavored gelatin, ¾ cup sugar, 1 cup water, and dash salt; heat till gelatin dissolves. Add ½ teaspoon grated orange peel and 1 cup orange juice; chill till partially thickened. Beat till fluffy; stir in 2 cups milk. Pour into 2-quart refrigerator tray. Freeze till firm. Makes about 1½ quarts.

SPICED CHERRY SAUCE

1 1-pound 4-ounce can frozen
tart red cherries, thawed
1 cup light corn syrup
½ cup sugar
3 tablespoons lemon juice
¼ teaspoon ground allspice
¼ teaspoon ground cloves
¼ teaspoon ground cinnamon

Drain cherries, reserving syrup. Combine cherry syrup with remaining ingredients and dash salt; bring to boil. Reduce heat; simmer 15 minutes; stir frequently. Remove from heat; stir in cherries. Cool. Makes 2½ cups.

Serve scoops of ice cream in a large bowl →
and let everyone make their own super
sundae with Spiced Cherry Sauce, nuts.

APRICOT-CHERRY SAUCE

Combine one 12-ounce jar (1 cup) apricot preserves and ½ cup red maraschino cherries, coarsely chopped. Makes 1½ cups.

RASPBERRY MELBA SAUCE

Thaw one 10-ounce package frozen raspberries. Blend 1½ teaspoons cornstarch with 1 tablespoon juice from raspberries till smooth. Sieve raspberries into saucepan; add ½ cup currant jelly; heat to boiling. Stir in cornstarch mixture. Cook and stir till thick and clear. Cool. Makes 1½ cups.

APPLE-CINNAMON SAUCE

In small saucepan, combine one 10-ounce jar apple jelly, 2 tablespoons red cinnamon candies, and ¼ cup water. Heat and stir till candies dissolve and jelly melts. Remove from heat; cool. Makes about 1 cup.

To make *Rainbow Parfait:* Pour small amount of sauce in bottom of each parfait glass. Layer sauce with flavors of sherbet.

PLUM SAUCE

1 12-ounce jar plum preserves
¼ cup port
1 teaspoon lemon juice *or*
¼ teaspoon almond extract

Thoroughly combine preserves with port and lemon juice *or* almond extract in small bowl. Chill. Serve over vanilla ice cream. Makes about 1¼ cups sauce.

CHOCOLATE RAISIN SAUCE

1 1-ounce square unsweetened chocolate
12 regular marshmallows
¼ cup water
⅓ cup raisins

Combine all ingredients in heavy saucepan. Cook over medium heat till marshmallows and chocolate are melted. Blend well. Serve warm over ice cream. Makes ¾ cup.

PEACH-NUT SAUCE

1 4¾-ounce jar strained peaches
⅓ cup light corn syrup
1 teaspoon lemon juice
Dash ground cinnamon
1 tablespoon butter or margarine
¼ teaspoon vanilla
¼ cup broken pecan halves

In saucepan, combine first 4 ingredients. Cook over medium heat, stirring constantly, till mixture boils. Cook 1 to 2 minutes. Stir in butter and vanilla. Add pecans. Serve warm over ice cream. Makes ¾ cup.

SPRING FRUIT SAUCE

1 tablespoon cornstarch
2 tablespoons sugar
¼ cup light corn syrup
1 16-ounce package frozen sliced strawberries, thawed
1 tablespoon lemon juice
1 cup sliced bananas

Mix cornstarch and sugar in saucepan; stir in corn syrup. Add strawberries. Cook, stirring constantly, till slightly thickened. Add lemon juice; cool. Before serving, stir in bananas. Spoon into sherbet glasses; top with scoop of orange sherbet. Makes 2½ cups.

TROPICAL SUNDAE SAUCE

1 8¾-ounce can pineapple tidbits
1½ cups sugar
1½ tablespoons lemon juice
3 drops peppermint extract
2 medium oranges, peeled, sectioned, and seeded
½ cup green maraschino cherries, halved

Drain pineapple, reserving syrup; add enough water to syrup to make ½ cup. Cook sugar and syrup over low heat till thickened, about 12 minutes. Add lemon juice and extract; chill. Before serving, add fruits. Makes 2 cups.

Ice cream sauces include from top left: → Apricot-cherry, Raspberry Melba, Apple-cinnamon, Plum, Peach-nut, Spring Fruit.

SHERRIED DATE SAUCE

2 cups pitted dates
¾ cup light corn syrup
½ cup sherry
1 tablespoon chopped preserved
  ginger
1 teaspoon shredded orange peel

Cut dates lengthwise in quarters. Combine with remaining ingredients; cover and refrigerate at least 24 hours. Serve over ice cream. Makes about 2½ cups sauce.

MINCEMEAT SUNDAE SAUCE

½ cup sugar
½ cup orange juice
½ cup diced pared apple
1 cup prepared mincemeat
¼ cup chopped California walnuts
¼ cup chopped maraschino cherries

Combine all ingredients in a small saucepan. Bring to boiling point; simmer gently, uncovered, 10 minutes. Serve warm over vanilla ice cream. Makes about 2½ cups.

WAIKIKI SUNDAE

¼ cup mashed ripe banana
2 teaspoons lemon juice
½ cup orange marmalade
½ cup pineapple-apricot preserves
¼ teaspoon rum flavoring
  Vanilla ice cream
½ cup flaked coconut, toasted

Combine banana and lemon juice; add marmalade and preserves. Cook and stir 5 minutes over low heat. Remove from heat; stir in flavoring. Spoon warm sauce over ice cream. Sprinkle with coconut. Makes 1⅓ cups.

CHERRY SUNDAE SAUCE

Combine ½ cup sugar and 2 teaspoons cornstarch. Add to 2 cups quartered fresh dark sweet cherries in a saucepan. Heat and stir till sugar dissolves and mixture thickens slightly. Stir in 1 tablespoon lemon juice. Chill. Serve over ice cream. Makes 1⅔ cups.

BLUEBERRY SAUCE

1 cup sugar
2 tablespoons cornstarch
¼ teaspoon ground nutmeg
1 cup boiling water
2 cups fresh blueberries*
3 tablespoons lemon juice

Combine sugar, cornstarch, nutmeg, and dash salt in saucepan. Gradually add water; mix well. Cook, stirring constantly, till mixture thickens and boils; cook 2 minutes more. Add blueberries; return to boiling. Remove from heat and stir in lemon juice; cool. Makes about 3 cups sauce.

*Or, use one 10-ounce package frozen unsweetened blueberries, thawed, and drained. Increase cornstarch to 3 tablespoons. Stir in blueberries with lemon juice (do not heat).

GOLDEN APRICOT SAUCE

1 1-pound 14-ounce can apricot
  halves
¾ cup sugar
¼ cup orange juice
½ teaspoon almond extract

Drain apricots, reserving ½ cup syrup. Cut up apricots and stir in reserved syrup, sugar, orange juice, and dash salt. Simmer 10 minutes; stir occasionally. Stir in extract; chill. Serve over ice cream. Makes 2 cups.

FRUIT SPARKLE SAUCE

1 1-pound 14-ounce can (3½ cups)
  fruit cocktail
¼ cup sugar
1 tablespoon cornstarch
¼ teaspoon salt
¼ cup water
½ 6-ounce can (⅓ cup) frozen
  orange juice concentrate, thawed
¼ cup coarsely chopped pecans

Drain fruit cocktail, reserving syrup. In a saucepan, combine sugar, cornstarch, and salt; blend in water. Add syrup and concentrate. Cook and stir till mixture thickens and boils. Add fruit; chill. Stir in pecans. Serve over vanilla ice cream. Makes 3½ cups.

BLUEBERRY SHAKE

    1 1-pound 5-ounce can blueberry
      or cherry pie filling
    2 pints vanilla ice cream
    1 cup milk
    4 teaspoons lemon juice

Place pie filling, ice cream, milk, and lemon juice in mixing bowl*; blend well. (For thinner shake, blend in an additional ½ cup milk.) Pour into 4 chilled tall glasses.

*For blender, divide recipe for 2 batches.

CITRUS COOLER

Pour ¼ cup frozen orange-grapefruit juice concentrate, thawed, into electric blender container. Add ¾ cup icy cold water and 1 pint lemon sherbet. Cover; blend 15 seconds. Divide mixture among 4 chilled glasses. Slowly pour in chilled ginger ale to fill each glass (one 12-ounce bottle is enough for this recipe). Stir gently; serve *immediately*.

PEACH-PINEAPPLE SHAKE

    1 cup sliced fresh peaches
    ¼ cup unsweetened pineapple juice,
      chilled
    ¼ cup sugar
    1 pint vanilla *or* peach ice cream
    ¾ cup milk

Place first 3 ingredients in electric blender container. Blend at high speed till smooth (about 10 seconds). Add ice cream; blend till softened. Add milk, mixing till blended. Pour into chilled tall glasses. Serve *immediately*. Fruit trim: String peach slices and maraschino cherries on straws. Serves 2.

FRUIT FLIP

Combine ½ cup fresh red raspberries, ½ cup diced ripe banana, ½ cup diced ripe peaches, ½ cup unsweetened pineapple juice, and ¼ cup sugar. Divide among four 8-ounce glasses; chill. For each glass: Add scoop of vanilla ice cream; muddle. Tip glass; slowly pour lemon-lime carbonated beverage down side. Add second scoop of ice cream.

MINTED SUNDAE SODA

    1 10-ounce jar mint-apple jelly
    ½ cup water
    1 quart vanilla ice cream
    1 pint lime sherbet
    2 12-ounce bottles (3 cups) lemon-
      lime carbonated beverage

In saucepan, combine mint-apple jelly and the water. Cook and stir over low heat till jelly melts. Cool to room temperature; then chill. Chill 6 to 8 large glasses; into each, pour 2 to 3 tablespoons mint jelly syrup. Add a spoonful of vanilla ice cream to each; stir till melted. Add a scoop of vanilla ice cream, then a scoop of lime sherbet, and top with another scoop of vanilla ice cream. Fill with lemon-lime carbonated beverage, pouring carefully down side of glass. Garnish each glass with a sprig of fresh mint or a thin slice of lime. Makes 6 to 8 servings.

BLENDER STRAWBERRY SODA

    1 cup boiling water
    1 3-ounce package strawberry-
      flavored gelatin
    1 quart milk
    1 quart vanilla ice cream

Pour water and gelatin in electric blender container. Blend till gelatin dissolves. Pour out ½ cup of the mixture. To remainder in blender add *half* the milk; blend well. Add *half* the ice cream; blend just till smooth. Pour into tall glasses. Repeat with remaining ingredients. Serves 6 to 8.

ROSY RASPBERRY FIZZ

    2 cups unsweetened pineapple juice
    1 10-ounce package frozen
      raspberries, partially thawed
    1 pint vanilla ice cream
    1 pint raspberry sherbet
    1 16-ounce bottle cream soda

Combine all ingredients except cream soda in large mixing bowl. Beat till blended; slowly pour in cream soda, mixing with up-and-down motion. Serve *immediately* in tall glasses. Makes 6 to 8 servings.

PLUM PARFAITS

    1 pound purple plums
    1 tablespoon cornstarch
    ¾ cup sugar
      Dash salt
      Dash ground cinnamon
      Dash ground cloves
    1 tablespoon lemon juice
      Vanilla ice cream

Rinse plums; slice, removing pits; measure 3 cups. Combine cornstarch, sugar, and salt in saucepan; stir in plums, spices, and lemon juice. Cover and bring to boil. Simmer 8 to 10 minutes; cool. Layer with vanilla ice cream in parfait glasses. Makes 4 to 6 servings.

CHERRY CREME PARFAITS

Whip 1 cup whipping cream with 3 tablespoons sugar, 1 teaspoon vanilla, and dash salt. Fold in 1 cup dairy sour cream. Alternate layers of one 1-pound 5-ounce can cherry pie filling and whipped cream mixture in parfait glasses; chill. Serves 8 to 10.

BIG APPLE PARFAITS

    1¼ cups boiling water
    1 3-ounce package raspberry-
      flavored gelatin
    1 1-pound can (1¾ cups)
      applesauce
    2 tablespoons lemon juice
    2 egg whites
      Dash salt
    ¼ cup sugar
      Vanilla ice cream

Add boiling water to gelatin; stir to dissolve gelatin. Add applesauce and lemon juice. Chill till partially set. Beat egg whites with salt till soft peaks form. Gradually add sugar, beating till stiff peaks form. Fold into gelatin mixture. Alternately spoon gelatin mixture and vanilla ice cream into parfait glasses. Top each with whipped cream. Serve immediately. Serves 6.

← Fresh purple plums take on a ruby glow in Plum Parfaits. The sauce is subtly spiced and lemon accented. Plum perfect!

LIME-BERRY PARFAITS

    1 3-ounce package lime-flavored
      gelatin
    1 cup boiling water
    1 8-ounce package cream cheese,
      softened
    ⅓ cup sugar
    ¼ cup orange juice
    ½ teaspoon grated lime peel
    3 tablespoons lime juice
    1 cup whipping cream, whipped
    1 10-ounce package frozen red
      raspberries, thawed

Dissolve gelatin in boiling water. Beat together cream cheese and sugar. Gradually add gelatin, orange juice, lime peel and juice to cream cheese mixture, beating till smooth. Chill till slightly thickened. Fold in whipped cream; chill till partially thickened. Alternate gelatin mixture and raspberries with syrup in parfait glasses. Serves 6.

CRAN-MELON PARFAITS

    1 1-pound can jellied cranberry
      sauce
    1 7-ounce bottle (about 1 cup)
      lemon-lime carbonated beverage
    1 medium honeydew melon, halved,
      seeded, and scooped into balls

Turn cranberry sauce into mixing bowl; beat till sauce is smooth. Resting bottle on rim of bowl, slowly pour in lemon-lime beverage. Mix gently with up-and-down motion. Pour into 1-quart refrigerator tray; freeze. Break into chunks; turn into chilled mixing bowl. Beat till fluffy. Return to tray and freeze. Layer cranberry ice and honeydew balls in 4 chilled parfait glasses. Serves 4.

CRANBERRY PARFAITS

Combine ½ cup sugar and 2 tablespoons cornstarch in saucepan. Add 2 cups cranberry-juice cocktail, 1 tablespoon lemon juice, dash aromatic bitters, and dash salt. Cook and stir over medium heat till thick; cool. Layer ice creams—strawberry, mai tai, Burgundy cherry, or boysenberry—in parfait glasses with cranberry sauce. Serves 6 to 8.

CANNING
AND
FREEZING

*A colorful trio of Cinnamon-
apple Jelly, Mint-
apple Jelly, and Apricot-
pineapple Jam
can be stored on the shelf
for use later or
given as hostess gifts.*

Home-style jams, jellies

CANNING PROCEDURES

Jelly tests: Dip large metal spoon into mixture; tilt spoon until syrup runs over side. When jellying stage is reached, liquid will stop flowing in a stream and divide in two distinct drops that run together and sheet from the edge of spoon. On thermometer, the temperature should register 8° higher than the boiling point of water. (Find the temperature at which water boils in your area—boiling point differs with altitude.)

Sealing jellies, jams, preserves: Cover hot jelly (not preserves or soft jams) immediately with enough hot paraffin to make a layer ⅛ inch thick. Prick any air bubbles.

Melt paraffin in a double boiler. Never let paraffin reach smoking temperatures.

Omit paraffin if using canning jars and lids. Tapered jars with straight sides are good for jelly and make it easy to slip jelly out in a molded shape. For jams and preserves, any type of canning jar may be used. Prepare lids according to manufacturer's directions. Fill hot scalded jars with boiling hot mixture. Wipe top and threads of jar clean. Place lid on jar; seal at once. Screw band tight.

Cooling and storing: Let jellies and jams stand undisturbed overnight. Cover paraffined jars (do not use lid that makes tight seal). Label; store in cool, dry, dark place.

APPLE-ORANGE MARMALADE

1 orange
5 cups sugar
2 tablespoons lemon juice*
8 cups thinly sliced tart apples
   (about 3 pounds)

Quarter orange, remove seeds, and slice very thin. Heat 1½ cups water and sugar till dissolved. Add lemon juice, orange, and apples. Boil rapidly, stirring constantly, till mixture thickens, 12 to 15 minutes. Remove from heat; ladle into hot scalded canning jars. Seal at once. After jars cool 30 minutes, shake gently to distribute fruit. Makes 3 pints.

*If apples are not tart, increase lemon juice to 3 tablespoons.

CINNAMON-APPLE JELLY

4 cups apple juice
1 2½-ounce package powdered
   fruit pectin
   Red food coloring
4½ cups sugar
3 to 4 tablespoons red cinnamon
   candies

Combine apple juice, pectin, and several drops food coloring in very large saucepan. Bring to hard boil. Stir in sugar and candies. Bring again to full *rolling boil; boil hard 2 minutes,* stirring constantly. Remove from heat and skim. Pour into hot scalded jars; seal at once. Makes about 8 glasses.

MINT-APPLE JELLY

Follow directions for Cinnamon-apple Jelly except combine 6 drops green food coloring and 1 cup lightly packed fresh mint leaves with apple juice and pectin. Omit red food coloring and cinnamon candies. Remove leaves before pouring into hot jars.

PEACH RUM JAM

3 pounds fully ripe peaches,
   scalded, peeled, and finely
   chopped (4 cups chopped)
1 1¾-ounce package powdered
   fruit pectin
      • • •
5 cups sugar
¼ cup light rum

Combine peaches and pectin in a very large saucepan or Dutch oven. Place over high heat and bring to a full rolling boil, stirring constantly. Immediately add all the sugar and stir. Again bring to a *full rolling boil and boil hard for 1 minute,* stirring constantly. Remove from heat; stir in rum. Skim off foam with metal spoon. Stir and skim for 5 minutes to cool slightly and prevent floating fruit. Ladle into hot scalded jars or glasses. Seal at once. Makes six to seven ½-pint jars.

CRAN-PINEAPPLE JELLY

3 cups cranberry-juice cocktail
1 cup unsweetened pineapple juice
⅓ cup lemon juice
1 1¾-ounce package powdered
    fruit pectin
5 cups sugar

Combine fruit juices with pectin in very large saucepan; stir over high heat till mixture boils hard. At once, stir in sugar. Bring to *full rolling boil; boil hard 1 minute*, stirring constantly. Remove from heat; skim off foam. Pour into 6 to 8 hot scalded jelly glasses, leaving ½-inch space at top. Seal at once. Makes 6 to 8 glasses.

BLUEBERRY MARMALADE

Remove peel from 1 medium orange and 1 lemon. Scrape excess white from peel; cut peel in *very fine* shreds. Place in very large saucepan. Add ¾ cup water. Bring to boil; simmer, covered, 10 minutes; stir occasionally. Remove white membrane on fruit; finely chop pulp (discard seeds). Add to peel with 3 cups crushed blueberries. Cover; simmer 12 minutes. Add 5 cups sugar. Bring to *full rolling boil; boil hard 1 minute*, stirring constantly. Remove from heat; immediately stir in *one-half* 6-ounce bottle liquid fruit pectin. Skim off foam; stir and skim for 7 minutes. Ladle into hot scalded jars. Seal at once. Makes six ½-pint jars marmalade.

GINGERED RHUBARB JAM

4 cups diced fresh rhubarb
3 cups sugar
3 tablespoons finely snipped
    candied ginger
2 tablespoons lemon juice
    Few drops red food coloring

Combine rhubarb with next 3 ingredients in large saucepan; let stand about 15 minutes or till sugar is moistened by juice. Cook over medium-high heat, stirring frequently till thick and clear, 12 to 15 minutes. Skim off foam; add red food coloring, if desired. Ladle into hot scalded jars or glasses. Seal at once. Makes three ½-pint jars jam.

CHERRY-STRAWBERRY JAM

1 1-pound 4-ounce can pitted tart
red cherries (water pack)
1 10-ounce package frozen sliced
strawberries, thawed
4½ cups sugar
3 tablespoons lemon juice
½ 6-ounce bottle liquid fruit
pectin

Drain cherries; reserve juice. Chop cherries; measure and add enough juice to make 2 cups. Combine cherries, strawberries, sugar, and lemon juice in large saucepan. Bring to *full rolling boil; boil hard 1 minute*, stirring constantly. Remove from heat; stir in pectin at once. Skim off foam. Stir and skim for 5 minutes to prevent fruit from floating. Ladle quickly into hot scalded jars. Seal at once. Makes six ½-pint jars.

PLUM JAM

4½ cups (about 2½ pounds) plums
7½ cups sugar
½ 6-ounce bottle liquid fruit
pectin

Wash plums, cut in pieces, and remove pits. Crush fruit and measure. Combine plums and sugar in large pan; bring to a *full rolling boil, stirring constantly. Boil hard for 1 minute*. Remove from heat; add pectin at once. Skim off foam and alternately skim and stir jam for 5 minutes to prevent fruit from floating. Ladle into hot scalded glasses and seal at once. Makes eight ½-pint glasses.

CHERRY MARMALADE

2 medium oranges
1 quart pitted dark sweet cherries
3½ cups sugar
½ cup lemon juice

Slice unpeeled oranges paper-thin; discard any seeds. Barely cover orange slices with cold water; cook till soft. Add cherries, sugar, and lemon juice. Simmer till thick and clear. Skim off foam and quickly ladle marmalade into hot scalded glasses. Seal at once. Makes about four ½-pint glasses.

STRAWBERRY-RHUBARB JAM

2 cups thinly sliced rhubarb
2 cups sliced fresh strawberries
2 tablespoons lemon juice
¼ teaspoon salt
1 1¾-ounce package powdered
fruit pectin
5½ cups sugar
12 drops red food coloring

Place first 5 ingredients in large saucepan; cook and stir till mixture comes to a fast boil; add sugar and stir. Add food coloring; bring *to full boil; boil hard 1 minute*, stirring constantly. Remove from heat; skim off foam and quickly pour into hot scalded glasses to ½ inch of top. Seal. Store in cool, dark place. Makes six ½-pint glasses.

APRICOT-PINEAPPLE JAM

Combine 6 cups fresh apricots, quartered, one 1-pound 4½-ounce can (2½ cups) crushed pineapple, and 4½ cups sugar. Bring to rolling boil, stirring constantly. Add one 4-ounce bottle (⅓ cup) maraschino cherries, drained and sliced. Boil hard, stirring constantly, till syrup sheets from spoon, about 15 minutes. Pour into hot scalded jars; seal immediately. Makes 4 pints.

THREE-FRUIT MARMALADE

4 medium oranges
4 pounds diced fresh peeled peaches
(8 cups)
4 pounds diced fresh pared pears
(8 cups)
1 1¾-ounce packaged powdered
fruit pectin
9 cups sugar

Slice unpeeled oranges in quarters, then in ¼-inch slices. Discard seeds. Measure fruits into large kettle and mix thoroughly. Cover and bring to a boil. Simmer gently 5 to 10 minutes. Stir in pectin and cook gently for 1 minute. Stir in sugar and bring to a vigorous boil, stirring constantly. *Boil hard 1 minute;* remove from heat. Skim and stir about 7 minutes. Pour into hot scalded jars. Seal at once. Makes 8 pints.

Orange and coconut give Peach Conserve a tropical flavor. It's tops on toast or rolls, and also over ice cream for an exotic sundae.

APPLE BUTTER

A beautiful russet color if made with a red apple—

6 pounds tart apples
6 cups cider or apple juice
3 cups sugar
2 teaspoons ground cinnamon
½ teaspoon ground cloves

Core and quarter apples (do not pare); cook in cider in a large, heavy saucepan till soft, about 30 minutes. Press through food mill.

Boil gently about 30 minutes; stir occasionally. Stir in sugar and spices. Cook and stir over low heat till sugar dissolves. Boil gently till mixture is desired thickness, about 1 hour. Stir frequently to avoid scorching. Pour into hot clean jars; adjust lids. Process jars 10 minutes (after water boils) in boiling water bath. Makes about eight ½-pints.

PEACH CONSERVE

2 pounds fully ripe peaches, scalded, peeled, and mashed (3 cups mashed)
1 6-ounce can frozen orange juice concentrate, thawed
5 cups sugar
1 6-ounce bottle liquid fruit pectin
1 3½-ounce can flaked coconut

Combine peaches and orange juice concentrate in a very large saucepan; stir in sugar. Bring mixture to a *full rolling boil; boil hard 1 minute*, stirring constantly. Remove from heat; immediately stir in liquid fruit pectin and coconut. Skim off foam with metal spoon. Stir and skim for 7 minutes. Ladle into hot scalded jars or glasses; seal at once. Makes seven ½-pint jars.

Canning fruit

ASSEMBLING EQUIPMENT

For good results, you will need canning equipment that's in tiptop shape!

Jars and lids must be flawless—no nicks, chips, or cracks. Use all new self-sealing lids or rubbers. If bail on glass-top jar is loose, remove bail; bend down in center; bend in sides to snap back in place.

Wash jars and lids, except those with sealing compounds, in sudsy water; rinse. Some metal lids with sealing compounds need boiling; others only a dip in hot water; follow manufacturer's directions.

Water-bath canner may be any big metal container with a cover and deep enough to have an inch or two of water over tops of jars and a little extra space for boiling. Use a rack to keep jars from touching bottom.

GLASS JAR CLOSURES

A flat metal lid with sealing compound and metal screw band fits the standard canning jar. When the band is screwed firmly, the lid has enough give to let air escape during processing. This lid is self-sealing—do not tighten further after processing.

Several kinds of two-piece metal caps are available. Follow manufacturer's directions.

In some areas you may find the porcelain-lined zinc screw cap with rubber ring that fits standard canning jars. In others, the wire-bail type of glass jar with glass lid and rubber ring is available. Tapered shoulderless jars use flat metal lids and screw bands.

YIELD OF CANNED FRUIT

Generally, for 1 quart canned fruit use the following amount of fresh fruit as purchased:

Fruit	Pounds
Apples	2½ to 3
Berries, except strawberries	1½ to 3
Cherries (if canned unpitted)	2 to 2½
Peaches	2 to 3
Pears	2 to 3
Plums	1½ to 2½

CANNING PROCEDURES

Most fruits may be canned two ways: cold pack (raw) or hot pack (precooked).

1. Wash jars and caps; rinse. Place in hot water till ready to fill jars. There's no need to sterilize jars—processing takes care of that. Place water bath canner on heat with enough water to cover jars over top.

2. Prepare fruit—see chart on next page.

3. Pack fruit into jars using either cold or hot pack method. Use syrup to suit sweetness of the fruit and your taste.

Cold pack: (May be used for all fruits except apples, applesauce, and rhubarb.) Pack fruit firmly into jars. Leave ½-inch headspace at top of jar. Pour boiling syrup into jars still leaving ½ inch headspace.

Hot pack: (May be used for all fruits.) Precook fruit in syrup according to directions in chart. Pack boiling hot fruit loosely into jars leaving ½ inch headspace (leave ¼ inch headspace for applesauce). Cover with boiling syrup still leaving the same headspace.

4. Chase out air bubbles from filled jars by working blade of knife down sides of jars. This helps keep liquid above food. Add more liquid if needed, but keep the headspace.

5. Wipe sealing edge of jars with clean cloth to remove food particles. Adjust jar caps. For self-sealing caps, put flat metal lid on jar with composition next to glass; screw the band tight. Partially seal jars with rubber rings and zinc caps by screwing caps down firmly, then turning caps back ¼ inch. For glass-top jars, click the longer wire over top of lid; leave shorter wire up.

6. Lower jars into water bath canner (have water hot but not boiling). Be sure jars do not touch. Cover. Count time when water comes to rolling boil. Keep water boiling gently during entire time. Add more *boiling* water if needed to keep jars covered.

7. Process for time indicated in chart. Processing times apply to food prepared at sea level. To correct time for high altitudes: Add 1 minute to processing time, if time specified is 20 minutes or less, for each 1,000 feet above sea level. Add 2 minutes for every 1,000 feet above sea level if processing time called for is more than 20 minutes.

Canning guide

Preparation

Fruit	Thin Syrup—2 cups sugar to 4 cups water. Yield 5 cups. Medium Syrup—3 cups sugar to 4 cups water. Yield 5½ cups. Heavy Syrup—4¾ cups sugar to 4 cups water. Yield 6½ cups. (Boil sugar and water together 5 minutes. Skim if needed. You'll need ½ to 1½ cups syrup for each quart jar.)	Water bath in minutes (pints)	Water bath in minutes (quarts)
Apples	*Hot Pack:* Pare, core, and cut in pieces. Treat to prevent darkening with ascorbic acid color keeper following package directions. Rinse; drain. Boil in syrup or water 5 minutes. Pack hot; cover with boiling syrup or water leaving ½ inch headspace. Adjust lids; process in boiling water bath.	15	20
	Applesauce: Prepare sauce; pack hot into hot jars leaving ¼-inch headspace. Adjust lids; process in boiling water bath.	10	10
Apricots Peaches Pears	*Cold Pack:* Wash and peel fruit (dip peaches and apricots in boiling water, then in cold water for easier peeling; *or* omit peeling apricots, if desired). Halve or slice; pit or core. Treat with ascorbic acid color keeper following package directions. Rinse; drain. Pack into hot jars; cover with boiling syrup leaving ½ inch headspace. Adjust lids; process in boiling water bath.	25	30
	Hot Pack: Prepare as above. Heat through in syrup. Pack hot into hot jars; cover with boiling syrup leaving ½-inch headspace. Adjust lids; process in boiling water bath.	20	25
Berries (except Strawberries)	*Cold Pack:* Use for raspberries, other soft berries. Fill hot jars. Cover with boiling syrup leaving ½-inch headspace. Adjust lids; process in boiling water bath.	10	15
	Hot Pack: Use for firm berries. Wash; drain. Add ½ cup sugar to each quart berries. Bring to boil in covered pan; shake pan to keep berries from sticking. Pack hot into hot jars leaving ½-inch headspace. Adjust lids; process in boiling water bath.	10	15
Cherries	*Cold Pack:* Wash, stem, and pit, if desired. Fill hot jars. Cover with boiling syrup leaving ½-inch headspace. Adjust lids; process in boiling water bath.	20	25
	Hot Pack: Wash; remove pits, if desired. Add ½ cup sugar to each quart fruit and a little water only to *unpitted* cherries. Cover; bring to boiling. Pack hot into hot jars leaving ½-inch headspace. Adjust lids; process in boiling water bath.	10	15
Plums	*Cold Pack:* Wash; prick skins if canning whole fruit. Halve and pit free-stone plums, if desired. Pack into hot jars. Cover with boiling syrup leaving ½-inch headspace. Adjust lids; process in boiling water bath.	20	25
	Hot Pack: Prepare as above. Bring to boil in syrup. Pack hot into hot jars; add boiling syrup leaving ½-inch headspace. Adjust lids; process in boiling water bath.	20	25
Rhubarb	*Hot Pack:* Wash; cut into ½-inch pieces. Add ½ cup sugar to each quart rhubarb; let stand to draw out juice. Bring to boil; pack hot into hot jars leaving ½-inch headspace. Adjust lids; process.	10	10

Sealing and cooling. Do not tighten self-sealing caps. Seal jars with jar rubbers and zinc caps immediately by screwing lid down tight. Seal glass-top jars by lowering short wire. If liquid boiled out, *do not open jar;* seal as is. Cool upright on cloth or rack.

Testing seal. Check seal on jars when cold.

To test jar with flat metal lid, press center of lid; if lid is drawn down, jar is sealed. Other types of caps won't leak when jar is tipped. If jar isn't sealed, use immediately; or check jar for flaws; reprocess with new lid.

Storing. Wipe jars; label with contents and date. Store in cool, dry, dark place.

Freezing fruit

FREEZING PROCEDURES

The intended use determines which freezing method is best. Syrup pack fruits are good for dessert; sugar pack, for cooking. Unsweetened fruit is generally lower quality, but is handy for special diet cookery.

Preparation: Freeze ripe fruits soon after harvesting. Prepare fruits for syrup or sugar pack as indicated in chart (page 147). Unsweetened pack method is at right.

Packaging: Moisture-vaporproof containers are essential. Rigid containers are: glass, aluminum, plastic, heavily waxed cardboard, or tin. Bags and sheets made of moisture-vaporproof materials as heavy foil, cellophane, plastic, or laminated papers are suitable. Pack fruit tightly to eliminate air.

Sealing: Leave headspace—room between the packed fruit and top of the container (see chart at right). This allows food to expand during freezing. Place piece of crumpled parchment paper atop fruit in container to hold fruit under juice. Follow manufacturer's directions for closing and sealing containers. Label with contents and date packed.

Freezing: Freeze at 0° or below in small batches. Keep fruits stored at this temperature until ready to use. Most fruits may be stored 8 to 12 months. Do not refreeze.

YIELD OF FROZEN FRUIT

Generally the following amount of fruit as purchased will yield 1 pint frozen fruit.

Fruit	Amount
Apples	1¼ to 1½ pounds
Apricots	⅔ to 4/5 pound
Berries*	1⅓ to 1½ pints
Cherries, sour	1¼ to 1½ pounds
Peaches	1 to 1½ pounds
Pears	1 to 1¼ pounds
Plums	1 to 1½ pounds
Raspberries	1 pint
Rhubarb	⅔ to 1 pound
Strawberries	⅔ quart

*Includes blackberries, blueberries, boysenberries, elderberries, huckleberries, and loganberries.

UNSWEETENED PACK

Apples: Follow directions for sugar pack (see chart, page 147), omitting sugar. Leave ½ inch headspace. Seal, label, and freeze.

Blueberries: Follow directions for syrup pack (see chart, page 147), omitting syrup. Leave ½ inch headspace. Seal; label; freeze.

Peaches and Strawberries: Wash, pit, and peel peaches; halve or slice. Wash, drain, hull berries; leave whole or slice. Fill separate containers (do not use glass). Cover with water containing 1 teaspoon crystalline ascorbic acid per quart. Leave ½ inch headspace in pints, 1 inch in quarts. Seal; freeze.

Plums: Wash. Pack whole into containers leaving ½ inch headspace; seal; freeze.

Raspberries: Wash; drain. Seal in containers; leave ½ inch headspace; freeze.

Rhubarb: Follow directions for syrup pack (see chart, page 147), omitting syrup. Leave ½ inch headspace. Seal, label, and freeze.

SYRUP PROPORTIONS

For syrup pack fruit: Add sugar to boiling water; stir to dissolve; chill. Figure ½ to ⅔ cup syrup for each pint package of fruit.

Syrup	Sugar (cups)	Water (cups)	Yield (cups)
Thin	2	4	5
Medium	3	4	5½
Heavy	4¾	4	6½
Very heavy	7	4	7¾
Extra heavy	8¾	4	8⅔

HEADSPACE

Leave the following headspace between fruit-syrup mixture and top of container:

Syrup or Sugar Pack			
Wide top opening		Narrow top opening	
Pint	Quart	Pint	Quart
½ inch	1 inch	¾ inch	1½ inches

See Unsweetened Pack for headspace.

Freezing guide

Fruit	Syrup Pack	Sugar Pack
Apples	Wash, pare, and core. Add $\frac{1}{2}$ teaspoon crystalline ascorbic acid to each quart Medium Syrup. Slice apples into $\frac{1}{2}$ cup cold syrup in container. Press down; cover with syrup; leave headspace. Seal; label; freeze.	Wash, pare, core, and slice. Steam slices $1\frac{1}{2}$ to 2 minutes; cool; drain. Sprinkle $\frac{1}{2}$ cup sugar over each quart of fruit; stir. Pack tightly into containers, leaving headspace. Seal, label, and freeze.
Apricots	Wash, halve, and pit. Peel and slice, if desired. If not peeled, cook in boiling water $\frac{1}{2}$ minute; cool; drain. Add $\frac{3}{4}$ teaspoon crystalline ascorbic acid to each quart Medium Syrup. Pack fruit tightly into containers. Cover with cold syrup; leave headspace. Seal; label; freeze.	Wash, halve, and pit. Peel and slice, if desired. If not peeled, cook in boiling water $\frac{1}{2}$ minute; cool; drain. Dissolve $\frac{1}{4}$ teaspoon crystalline ascorbic acid in $\frac{1}{4}$ cup cold water; sprinkle over 1 quart apricots. Mix $\frac{1}{2}$ cup sugar with each quart fruit; stir till dissolved. Pack into containers, pressing down till juice covers fruit. Leave headspace; seal; label; freeze.
Blueberries Elderberries Huckleberries	Wash; drain. Steam 1 minute; cool quickly. Pack into containers; cover with cold Medium Syrup. Leave headspace; seal; freeze.	
Cherries, sour	Stem, wash, drain, and pit. Pack into containers; cover with cold Very Heavy or Extra Heavy Syrup, depending on tartness of fruit. Leave headspace; seal; label; freeze.	Stem, wash, drain, and pit. To each quart fruit add $\frac{3}{4}$ cup sugar; mix till dissolved. Pack into containers, leaving headspace. Seal, label, and freeze.
Peaches	Wash, pit, and peel (for smooth look, don't scald). Add $\frac{1}{2}$ teaspoon crystalline ascorbic acid per quart Medium Syrup. Slice peaches into $\frac{1}{2}$ cup syrup in container or leave in halves, press fruit down; add syrup to cover; leave headspace; seal; freeze.	Wash, pit, and peel (for smooth look, don't scald). Halve or slice. Dissolve $\frac{1}{4}$ teaspoon crystalline ascorbic acid in $\frac{1}{4}$ cup cold water. Sprinkle over 1 quart fruit; add $\frac{2}{3}$ cup sugar; mix well. Pack into containers; leave headspace; seal; label; freeze.
Pears	Wash, pare, halve or quarter and remove cores. Cook in boiling Medium Syrup for 1 to 2 minutes; drain; cool. Pack pears into containers. Add $\frac{3}{4}$ teaspoon crystalline ascorbic acid per quart Medium Syrup; cover fruit with syrup, leaving headspace. Seal, label, and freeze.	
Plums	Wash, halve or quarter; pack into containers. Add $\frac{1}{2}$ teaspoon crystalline ascorbic acid to each quart Medium or Heavy Syrup, depending on tartness. Cover fruit with syrup; leave headspace; seal; label; freeze.	
Raspberries Blackberries Loganberries Boysenberries	Wash and drain. Place in containers. Cover with cold Medium or Heavy Syrup, leaving headspace. Seal, label, and freeze.	Wash and drain. To 1 quart berries, add $\frac{3}{4}$ cup sugar; mix carefully to avoid crushing. Place in containers, leaving headspace. Seal, label, and freeze.
Rhubarb	Wash, trim, cut into 1 or 2 inch pieces or in lengths to fit container. Cook in boiling water 1 minute; cool in cold water. Pack into containers; cover with cold Medium Syrup; leave headspace; seal; label; freeze.	
Strawberries	Wash, drain, remove hulls. Slice or leave whole. Place in containers; cover with cold Heavy Syrup; leave headspace. Seal, label, and freeze.	Wash, drain, remove hulls. Slice or leave whole. Add $\frac{3}{4}$ cup sugar to each quart of berries; mix well. Place in containers, leaving headspace. Seal; label; freeze.

FRESH
FRUIT
RAISONNÉ

Apples by the bushel include crisp, juicy eating-out-of-hand Golden and Red Delicious, versatile Jonathans, Jonadels that are a cross of the two, and Pound Sweet.

Apples 'round the cider include—red-mottled
McIntosh in basket, ruby red Rome Beauty,
yellow Grimes Golden, Edgewood Jonathan.

APPLES—come in many different varieties and each has its own purpose and distinctive flavor. Some are best for baking, some for eating-out-of-hand or in salads, and others for general cooking—such as for sauce and cobblers. Some apples are sweet, some mellow, and others tart. Most varieties of apples are on the market from fall till early spring, but with modern methods of preservation in atmospherically controlled rooms, the seasons are being lengthened.

When buying apples, choose those with a good color for the variety for fullest flavor. The apples should be firm to the touch; apples that are overripe yield to slight pressure and will often be soft, mealy, and lacking in flavor.

Warm temperatures cause apples to lose crispness and tangy flavor; keep reserve supplies refrigerated.

Choose apples for their best use. For baking it's important to use apples that hold their shape but bake through such as Rome Beauty (thought by many to be the best baking apple) or Rhode Island Greening. For sauce, apples should be tart and juicy; good choices are Gravenstein and Rhode Island Greening. You can use most any all-purpose apple in a pie, but most cooks prefer a tart, juicy apple. The Baldwin is a choice pie apple.

All-purpose apples (eating, cooking, and baking) include Baldwin, Jonathan, McIntosh, Northern Spy, Stayman, Wealthy, Winesap, and Yellow Newton.

The best eating-out-of-hand or salad apple is the Delicious, either Red or Golden. These great apples are identified by five knobs on the blossom end. Grimes Golden and Gravenstein are also good for eating-out-of-hand or for salads.

AVOCADOS—vary in shape, size, color —from green to almost black. Small finger-like avocados are seedless.

When selecting an avocado, cradle it in the palm of the hand; if it yields to gentle pressure, it's ready to eat. (Or, insert wooden pick into stem end; when pick glides in easily, it's ripe.) To be at its best, an avocado must ripen till no feeling of firmness remains. Keep at room temperature till ripe; then refrigerate (up to 3 days) till needed.

To prepare, halve lengthwise and twist gently to separate. Twist and lift out seed. Loosen skin and strip from fruit, starting at narrow end. Brush with citrus juice to keep fruit from darkening.

RASPBERRIES—red, purple, and black, are tender fruits and require careful handling. Look for berries that are bright, clean, fresh in appearance, and have full color for the variety of berry. The berries should be plump and not soft or leaky, which often results from bruising and crushing.

Avoid berries that have the caps attached. Usually if the caps adhere firmly, they are not mature berries. A berry that has all of its cells showing a normal ripe color will have much better flavor than one with green or off-color cells.

Blackberries and dewberries are elongated. Both are larger, black, and have larger seeds than raspberries.

GOOSEBERRIES—will be soft and have a light amber color when ripe. Remove tiny stems and bloom ends.

STRAWBERRIES—should be free from white, green, or hard black tips and should have caps attached. Size, varying with variety, is not always indicative of good flavor. Swirl berries (with caps on) through water just before using; hull.

CURRANTS—may be red, black, or white. Avoid overripe (soft) currants for jelly-making as they do not "jell" as well.

BLUEBERRIES—are similar to huckleberries but are usually larger than huckleberries and have small inconspicuous seeds. The bloom depends upon variety as does color—blue, black, or purplish.

GRAPEFRUIT—the Marsh seedless, the Duncan, and the pink-meated grapefruit, are the most marketed varieties. Choose fruits that are firm, well-shaped, and heavy for their size. Heaviness is a good indication of high juice content. Color ranges from pale yellow to russet.

LEMONS—should be moderately firm, be heavy for size, and have fine-textured, waxy skin. Soft lemons are undesirable.

LIMES—that are green, are more acid than the yellow-colored ones. They should be heavy for their size.

KUMQUATS—are always small, thin-skinned, and orange-like. Both rind and pulp are edible.

TANGERINES—look like small, flattened oranges and are easier to peel. Fruits should be firm, not puffy.

TANGELOS—are a cross between the tangerine and grapefruit, have juicy pulp, and are easily peeled.

ORANGES—Navel and Valencia are the leading varieties. Navels are seedless, slightly thick skinned, and are easy to peel and segment. They are known as eating oranges. Valencia oranges have several seeds, a smooth skin, and thin membranes. They are good for juicing.

Look for oranges that are heavy for their size (this indicates lots of juice), firm, and with skins that are not too rough. Color is not always a sure guide to ripeness because some oranges have coloring added. (They must be stamped "Color Added" and must meet the standards of ripeness.) Late-season Valencias often have a greenish tinge, affecting only the skin; the fruit is matured, fully ripe, sweet, and juicy.

Temple oranges are one of the most attractive fruits in the citrus family. They are very juicy, easy to peel, and have a spicy, rich flavor.

Citrus fruits arranged in basket are Navel oranges, lemons, limes; from right base are Tangelos, Tangerines, white Marsh seedless and Ruby Red grapefruit, and Valencia oranges.

FIGS—vary in color from green to yellow, brown, purple, and black, when ripe, depending on the variety. Fully ripe fresh figs should be fairly soft to the touch. Figs are extremely perishable; overripeness can be detected by a sour odor.

Important varieties include dark purple Mission, large white Calimyrna, white Adriatic, and Kadota, a smaller white type.

Figs were one of the earliest fruits cultivated by man. Spanish missionaries first cultivated them in California. Today, domestic commercial fig growing is confined largely to California and Texas because of favorable climate. Imported figs come chiefly from Turkey, Greece, and Italy.

GRAPES—in basket include red-purple Cardinals, green Thompson Seedless, and the large, black, round Ribiers. The best U.S. crops come from two areas. Catawba, Concord, and Niagara grapes from eastern and central regions have skins that separate easily from the pulp but the seeds are hard to remove. Others most successfully grown in the West include Thompson Seedless, Flame Tokay, Red and White Malagas, Emperor, Ribier, and Cardinal grapes; they have reverse characteristics and are sweeter.

Choose well-formed grape clusters. Color is a guide to ripeness. Darker varieties should be free of green tinge; white grapes show a slight amber blush.

SANTA CLAUS or CHRISTMAS MELON weighs 6-9 pounds; has green and gold rind. Meat is in shades of green. Mild, slightly sweet flavor.

PERSIAN MELON—weighs 4-8 pounds. Gray netting on green rind; orange meat. Mildly sweet. Smooth stem end; pleasant aroma when ripe.

CASABA MELON — is mild and slightly sweet; soft, creamy white meat. Deeply furrowed; butter yellow.

CRANSHAW MELON—is a cross of Persian and Casaba. Meat is pink-orange, juicy, almost spicy; full aroma.

HONEYDEW MELON—has sweet and juicy meat—"almost melting" texture. Slightly waxy, rather fragile, creamy-yellow rind, pleasant aroma.

ICEBOX WATERMELON—is a midget weighing 6-10 pounds. Taste is surest guide to ripeness. Serve icy-cold. Should be symmetrical and firm.

APRICOTS—should be golden yellow, plump, fairly firm, and juicy. Avoid buying soft and shriveled apricots.

PEACHES—are either white- or yellow-fleshed and both types have clingstone and freestone varieties. Freestones are most popular for home canning, table, and general use; clingstones are chiefly for commercial canning. Background color should be whitish or yellowish, often with red blush. They should be plump and fairly firm. If picked too green, they won't ripen satisfactorily.

NECTARINES—look and taste like a peach without "fuzz". They are red, white, or yellow-fleshed and can be freestone or clingstone. Select as for peaches.

PEARS—should be ripened in a cool, dark place off the tree. When ripe, they will yield to gentle pressure at stem end.

In back basket with the Anjou is the Fall Russet (like Bosc), which has a long tapering neck, cinnamon-brown color, and sugar-sweet, spicy flavor. Firm-ripe ones can be baked. The heart-shaped Anjou pear has a smooth, thin, light green or creamy yellow skin when ripe.

The large pears in front basket are Comice. This is a sweet and juicy pear with creamy-yellow skin, often prized for holiday gifts (to be eaten as is). The shapely pears with red blush are Bartletts. They have smooth texture, are rich, juicy, and sweet—an all-purpose pear.

QUINCE—is a golden-yellow colored fruit resembling a yellow apple. It has a more acid-bitter flesh with many hard seeds, while the apple is sweeter. Pick those that are free from blemishes and firm. Handle gently because they are easily bruised. Quinces are a fall fruit and are used for jelly-making and preserving.

PRICKLY PEAR—is the fruit of a species of cactus with minute prickly spines. These spines can be easily removed by singeing before peeling the fruit. Prickly pears range in color from yellow to crimson on the outside and have a vivid purplish-red color inside and many hard seeds. Choose those that are firm and have a bright, fresh appearance.

The color of plums is not always a good indication of ripeness because plums vary in color according to the variety—from green to purple.

PLUMS—included in the picture (along front edge of basket from left) are El Capitan, Elephant Heart, Santa Rosa, Queen Ann, and Italian Prune; back row (from left) includes Ace, Kelsey, President, Mariposa, and El Dorado.

Versatile plums have a refreshing tartness that makes them good as is or used in prepared dishes such as pies, ice cream, and compotes. Choose plums that are plump, full colored, and soft enough to yield to slight pressure. Softening at the tip is usually a sign that the fruit is mature. Avoid plums that are shriveled and hard; they will have poor flavor.

Fresh prunes are a variety of plums which are suitable for drying. This type can be separated from the pit like a freestone peach; it is best for canning.

Damson plums are small, tart, purple plums used chiefly for jam and jelly.

MANGO—(at top opposite page) varies in size from a plum to an apple and has from yellow to red color, depending on variety. It has a smooth skin and is often speckled with black; it tastes like a combination of pineapple and apricot. Choose mangos that are solid and not too soft to the touch. Green mangos are often used for jams and chutneys.

KIWI—(at top opposite page) are sometimes called Chinese gooseberries. This fruit is imported from New Zealand. They are about the size of a lemon, oval-shaped, and have a brown fuzzy skin; they will be soft to the touch, like an avocado, when ripe. To serve, rub away the fuzz, halve, and drizzle with lemon or lime juice; spoon from the skin. Or, peel, cut up, and add to salads. They'll keep for weeks if refrigerated, but they should be at room temperature to ripen.

PAPAYA—is the melon-like tropical fruit with a pear shape. It has a thin, smooth skin and is green till ripe—then yellow. Its deep golden flesh is tender and rather buttery in texture, and there are hundreds of peppery-tasting black seeds that fill the center cavity. Papayas are distinctive—at once bland and mellow with a succulent fruit sweetness.

Look for greenish-yellow to full-yellow color, and flesh that will yield slightly when fruit is pressed in palm of hand. Ripen, if necessary, at room temperature out of direct sunlight. Refrigerate fully ripe fruit. To serve, slice lengthwise, remove seeds, and serve like a melon, with a lime wedge.

← **POMEGRANATE**—is often called "the apple with many seeds." This fruit is a colorful autumn-winter fruit that looks like an apple but has a hard, somewhat leathery skin. Those with thin skins of bright purply-red color and fresh appearance are best to buy. The skin encasing the fruit makes it a good keeper, too.

The crimson seeds and juice are the edible parts of the pomegranate. The seeds are crisp and juicy to bite into and have a slightly sweet, yet tangy flavor. Use them to add color and flavor accents to salads and desserts. The seeds are easily removed with a fork.

Grenadine syrup, used to flavor iced drinks, is made from pomegranate juice.

PERSIMMON—resembles a large ripe tomato in shape, and firmness—a true winter delicacy! A major difference from tomatoes is the stem cap of the persimmon, which should be attached when you purchase the fruit. The oriental variety, commonly found on the market, is astringent when green, but turns soft, rich, and sweet as it ripens.

When buying persimmons, look for those that are firm and shapely, plump, and highly colored (orange-red). After ripening in a cool, dark place, they should be refrigerated. Persimmons are very delicate, so handle them gently. Serve lime or lemon slices to accent the distinctive flavor of this fruit.

INDEX

A-B